Research Interviewing

Research Interviewing

Context and Narrative

Elliot G. Mishler

Harvard University Press
Cambridge, Massachusetts
and London, England

First Harvard University Press paperback edition, 1991

Library of Congress Cataloging-in-Publication Data
Mishler, Elliot George, 1924–
Research interviewing.

Bibliography: p.
Includes index.
1. Social surveys. 2. Interviewing. 3. Discourse
analysis. 4. Psychology—Research. I. Title.
HN29.M48 1986   301'.0723   86-9798
ISBN 0-674-76460-9 (alk. paper)
ISBN 0-674-76461-7 (pbk.)

*In memory of Nita
and for Mark and Renee, Paul, Gerrie and Max, and Vicky*

Preface

Interviews hold a prominent place among research methods in the social and behavioral sciences. In this book I examine current views and practices of interviewing and conclude that they reflect a restricted conception of the interview process. This view obscures the essence of interviewing—that it is an occasion of two persons speaking to each other—and undercuts the potential and special contribution of interviewing for theoretical understanding of human action and experience. I propose a reformulation of interviewing, one that attempts to redress the problems engendered by the standard approach. At its heart is the proposition that an interview is a form of discourse. Its particular features reflect the distinctive structure and aims of interviewing, namely, that it is discourse shaped and organized by asking and answering questions. An interview is a joint product of what interviewees and interviewers talk about together and how they talk with each other. The record of an interview that we researchers make and then use in our work of analysis and interpretation is a representation of that talk. How we make that representation and the analytic procedures we apply to it reveal our theoretical assumptions and presuppositions about relations between discourse and meaning.

This view of interviews now appears to me to be self-evident.

Nonetheless, it is not the view guiding most interview research. In the mainstream tradition, the idea of discourse is suppressed. Questions and answers, for example, are regarded as analogues of stimuli and responses rather than as forms of speech. This approach has led to massive efforts to standardize questions and interviewer behavior so that all respondents will receive the same "stimulus." The assumption that these efforts have succeeded underlies an elaborate technology of coding and statistical analysis. The suppression of discourse is accompanied by an equally pervasive disregard of respondents' social and personal contexts of meaning, both in the interview itself, where standardization overrules the particularities of individual and setting, and in the modes of interpretive theorizing about responses. Where issues of context are addressed, they are treated as technical problems rather than acknowledged as essential components of meaning-expressing and meaning-understanding processes.

These observations are documented and elaborated in the Introduction and Chapter 1 of this book. The survey research interview is my primary focus, for several reasons. First, it is the most well-developed and widely used interview method and can justifiably be considered the standard or mainstream approach. Second, the principal features of such interviews—for example, the standard format of interview schedules and the emphasis on fixed response categories combined with systematic sampling procedures, quantitative measures, and statistical methods—are regarded as close approximations to the dominant model of scientific research. Because of its presumed virtues in this regard, the survey interview tends to be used as the criterion for evaluating the adequacy of other approaches, such as clinical, ethnographic, and life-history interviewing. Thus, investigators using the latter approaches are often faulted for eschewing standardization of the interview situation and for not relying on statistical analysis of aggregated responses in interpreting their data.

My argument is advanced with close attention to empirical studies of the interview process, many of them conducted by survey researchers themselves, addressed to problems such as the effects on responses of variations in question wording, contexts, and interviewer characteristics and behaviors. I conclude from the results of these studies that the standard approach to interviewing is demonstrably inappropriate for and inadequate to the study of the central questions in the social and behavioral sciences, namely, how individuals perceive, organize, give meaning to, and express their understandings of themselves, their experiences, and their worlds. Further, the traditional approach neglects to examine how their understandings are related to their social, cultural, and personal circumstances.

The critique of standard practice sets the stage for an extended presentation of an alternative approach to research interviewing. This approach covers a family of methods varying in form and purpose but all embodying the view that an interview is a form of discourse. The contrast between this view and the assumptions of mainstream survey interviewing is used to develop a framework for systematic exposition of the alternative. Four propositions are specified as its essential components: (1) interviews are speech events; (2) the discourse of interviews is constructed jointly by interviewers and respondents; (3) analysis and interpretation are based on a theory of discourse and meaning; (4) the meanings of questions and answers are contextually grounded. In successive chapters each of these propositions and its implications for research practice are discussed.

As in the critique of the standard approach, the argument for the alternative is grounded in empirical examples, with special attention to transcripts of tape-recorded interviews and to methods for the analysis of speech. For example, in the discussion of the essential nature of interviews as a jointly constructed discourse, the ways that interviewers and interviewees arrive at a mutually shared understanding of the meanings of questions and responses are shown through examples of variations between interviewers and respondents in how "standard" questions are asked and the effects on responses of these differences. Chapter 4 shows, through presentation of several methods for the analysis of interviews as narrative accounts, how a theory of discourse and meaning enters into analysis and interpretation. In the Appendix, as a resource for further reading, I assemble and discuss approaches developed in various disciplines for the study of narratives in contexts other than interviews—for example, in literature, cultural rituals, history, psychoanalysis, as well as developmental and experimental research on cognition and language. Chapter 5, on contextual grounds of meaning, places interviewing in a larger sociocultural context and focuses specifically on the issue of effects on respondents of different types of interviewing practice. Using examples of studies that give a more participatory and collaborative role to respondents in the research process, I propose that research be guided by the aim of empowering respondents.

These themes are reviewed in the conclusion with reference to general issues of theory and research in the human sciences. My claim that interviewing is a particularly valuable method of inquiry, the basic presupposition of my argument, is explicitly linked to its distinctive merits for the study of discourse and meaning. I suggest two preconditions for more widespread and fuller recognition among research scientists of its special strengths. First, the topics of discourse and meaning must be restored to a central place in our theoretical and empirical studies of human experience and action. Second, systematic methods must be developed for the conduct and analysis of interviews that preserve their essential features as discourse. The detailed exposition in Chapters 2 through 5 is designed to achieve these aims, that is, to satisfy both preconditions and thereby to demonstrate how the potential strengths of interviewing can be realized in practice.

This book reflects my long-standing interest in the assumptions and implications of alternative research methods in the human sciences. The central ideas around which it revolves emerged gradually from my own studies, from teaching, and from the give-and-take of talk among friends, colleagues, and students. Their contributions are only partially and inadequately recognized by formal acknowledgment here.

I have learned a great deal from the independent work of several postdoctoral research fellows. Marianne Paget's studies of in-depth interviewing deepened my awareness of the significance of interviewing as a method and sensitized me to a variety of issues in the interpretation of relations between speech and meaning. Susan Bell's efforts to develop systematic methods of analyzing interviews as narrative accounts has directly informed my own work on this problem. Her critical and constructive comments on earlier drafts of this work helped clarify both my thoughts and their exposition.

Discussions of various approaches to interviewing in my research seminar over the past few years brought many problems into sharper focus. For their serious attention and for their many suggestions, I am pleased to thank Tim Anderson, Barbara Dickey, Darlene Douglas-Steele, Peter Goldenthal, Linda Isaacs, Kyung Kim, Daniel Kindlon, Marianne LaFrance, Thomas Schweitzer, Sally Tarbell, Joanne Veroff, and Joseph Veroff. My understanding of narratives and of various approaches to their analysis has also benefited from discussions of my work and that of others in the informal narrative study group at the Harvard School of Education, which has included Courtney Cazden, James Gee, Charles Haynes, Sarah Michaels, and Dennie Wolf.

Stuart Hauser, Sol Levine, Cathy Riessman, Vicky Steinitz, and Joseph Veroff each gave a close reading to an early draft of the manuscript. In the spirit of friendship they encouraged my efforts and combined their support with critical and detailed attention to various shortcomings, omissions, and ambiguities in my argument. The work is both stronger and clearer because of them.

Anita L. Mishler's influence on me is pervasive and immeasurable. The term *acknowledgment* cannot convey the sense in which her views and thoughts have entered my work. She died before this book took final shape, but much of what appears here reflects understandings we arrived at together. I have tried to show this at least in part by giving a place in these pages to some of her own work and to some of the work we did together.

I hope that those who have been responsive to earlier versions of this book will find the final version responsive to their advice and concerns. The faults that remain despite their efforts are, of course, my own.

Contents

Research Interviewing

Introduction: Problems of the Research Interview

In one of the earliest and still one of the most artful papers on interviewing as a research method, Paul Lazarsfeld (1935, p. 1) begins: "Asking for reasons and giving answers are commonplace habits of everyday life." Noting the difference between the routine nature of such habits and the situation of the research interview, he alludes to a critical problem: namely, the shared assumptions, contextual understandings, common knowledge, and reciprocal aims of speakers in everyday life are not present in the formal interview. The latter excludes exactly those factors that allow participants in the flow of ordinary discourse to understand directly and clearly what questions and answers mean. Lazarsfeld remarks that for these reasons, "in market research, the question-and-answer business is not so simple, and the ease of furnishing answers in everyday life may involve dangerous pitfalls."

Twenty years later, two other astute students of interviewing make a similar observation about both its ubiquity and its problems. Riesman and Benney (1956, p. 225) state that "every one in business—as in social life generally—is asking and answering questions all the time, whether or not this process is formalized and termed 'an interview.' " They, too, quickly add the caution that although interviewing is commonplace, "asking and answering questions is at once a simple and subtle affair, and we shall concentrate on the subtleties."

More recently, Schuman (1982, pp. 22–23), commenting on "both the strengths and weaknesses of survey research as a major force in 20th century social science," suggests that surveys have their origin in "two of our most natural intellectual inclinations. One is to ask questions of other people and treat their answers with some seriousness . . . The second inclination is to draw samples to represent a much larger universe." Like Lazarsfeld and Riesman and Benney before him, Schuman then refers to the problems that emerge from the formalization of this "natural" inclination into a research method: "But this blend of the natural and the sophisticated, which gives surveys their strengths, also contains weaknesses." Among the principal problems, he notes that "too much can be inferred from answers taken at face value to questions of dubious merit . . . all answers depend upon the way a question is formulated. Language is not a clean logical tool like mathematics that we can use with precision . . . As if this complexity were not enough, our answers are also influenced by who asks the question."

These observations span the period during which interviewing achieved mature status as a research method, particularly as it is exemplified in survey research. Clearly, they mark an awareness among some reflective investigators of a sharp disjunction or gap between asking and answering in naturally occurring conversations and the same process transformed into a systematic research procedure. Nonetheless, despite occasional references to the problem (such as those cited), the relationship between these two types of discourse has not received serious attention. As will become apparent, the exploration of how asking and answering in research interviews draws upon our everyday understanding and competence as language users is a leitmotiv of this book. The "gap" between the two modes of speech is therefore a useful point of departure for the critical analysis undertaken here of interviewing as a research practice.

How investigators have addressed, or failed to address, this problem reveals some central assumptions of the mainstream tradition of survey research interviewing, particularly those regarding the relationship between speech and meaning. Clarifying these assumptions and how they inform practice will help us specify the limitations of this approach and will guide us toward an alternative. A review of interview research reveals a paradox rather than total neglect: investigators rarely give the problem direct or analytic attention, but their practices evidence a high degree of indirect preoccupation with it. On the one hand, there is a deep silence about the gap and its implications, particularly with regard to how findings are interpreted and understood. On the other hand, many of the techniques developed for conducting and analyzing interviews represent efforts to ascertain the meaning of respondents' answers to questions in the absence of those contextual grounds of understanding, noted by Lazarsfeld, that are present in everyday conversations. These techniques include, for example, prescriptions and recommendations for constructing schedules, training interviewers, developing and applying codes, and using multivariate statistics. I am suggesting that the varied and complex procedures that constitute the core methodology of interview research are directed primarily to the task of making sense of what respondents say when the everyday sources of mutual understanding have been eliminated by the research situation itself.

This general point is elaborated in detail in the following chapters, and emphasis is placed on examination of the interview process and on the structure and meaning of questions and responses. At this point, to introduce some of the key issues and to foreshadow the main thrust of my argument, I will comment briefly on two typical steps in an interview study: coding and statistical analysis.

The central problem for coding may be stated as follows: because meaning is contextually grounded, inherently and irremediably, coding depends on the competence of coders as ordinary language users.[1] Their task is to determine the "meaning" of an isolated response to an isolated question, that is, to code a response that has been stripped of its natural social context. Their competence consists in their being able to restore the missing context. One hallmark of a good study is the quality of its coding manual. It must be sufficiently detailed for coders to distinguish categories and subcategories from each other in terms of their intended core definitions and their respective ranges of reference. At the same time it must be sufficiently abstract for codes to be applied to new responses that vary in specific features from the manual's exemplars. This is a delicate task. Rather than saying that coders *use* a manual, it would be more precise to say that they *interpret* it.

In this act of interpretation, coders rely on the varied assumptions and presuppositions they employ as ordinary language users. Although coders may share a common linguistic culture, there is considerable individual variation in frames of reference, values, levels of understanding. Experienced researchers know that however elaborate and elegant the coding manual and however explicit the rules for interpretation, the actual work of coding cannot be done reliably until coders build up a set of shared assumptions, specific to the study, that allow them to implement the code in a mutually consistent way. The development of such a coders' subculture is the most significant by-product of training and periodic reliability checks of coders. Often these assumptions are ad hoc, reflect coders' everyday understandings and competences as language users, and tend to remain tacit in the research process.

Emphasizing the significance of interpretive activity in coding, as I have done, is somewhat unusual, but I do not think that this characterization of the process would be disputed by other investigators. Rather, at issue here is how this understanding informs analysis and interpretation of interview data. On the whole, practitioners' knowledge of how coding is done tends to be put aside at the point of interpretation; coded responses are treated as if they were independent of the contexts that produced them. Yarrow and Waxler (1979, pp. 42–43), in a cogent analysis of problems of behavior-interaction coding that applies with equal force to interview-response coding, make a similar point: "Codes are generally defined in context-free, sequence free terms . . . In the service of developing agreements, coders establish conventions for determining the boundaries of each code, and for handling ambiguous events. Conventions can become too foolproof with everything fitted neatly into a set of categories ... Although a good deal of uncertainty often accompanies coding, even though agreement exists, once coding is accomplished, feelings of uncertainty about possibly miscalled behavior begins to subside. Statistical evidence brings assurance; significant relations are forthcoming, and findings appear."

In this way, awareness of the contextual grounds of meaning is suppressed, for both the interview responses and their code representations, and excluded from the interpretation of findings. The point I wish to underscore, and will repeat in various ways throughout this book, is that the practices exhibited in coding depend on implicit assumptions as to the relationship between meaning and language. The usual everyday sources of understanding are first stripped away through the research process, creating the gap referred to in the citations with which this chapter began. The result is an array of decontextualized responses. But because such responses have no "meaning" in themselves, everyday contextual understandings are reintroduced, slipped into the analysis through the back door of a coders' subculture. They are the invisible but necessary background of work. A central task of my argument is to make these assumptions visible, to bring them forward for critical reflection, and to suggest alternative forms of practice that take them more fully into account.

A related problem appears in the way that statistical analyses enter into interpretation. Techniques of multivariate statistics allow testing for significant differences across population subgroups, often distinguished from one another along social attributes, singly or in combination, such as gender, age, and social class. As is true of coding, interpretation of these differences relies on unexplicated assumptions about the "meanings" of questions and responses. For example, interpreting differences in the frequency among social classes of a particular response to a specific question depends on the assumption that the question "meant" the same thing to all respondents. (To anticipate an argument I will make later in more detail: it is assumed that all respondents received the same stimulus.) Excluded from this line of reasoning is the possibility of variation among subgroups in their understandings of questions and in the intentional meanings of answers in how these are, in turn, related to variation in sociocultural frameworks of language and meaning. There is little consideration of the problem that comparison groups may only partially share a common culture and that they in other respects may represent quite different subcultures. The particular combination of such partial over-laps would have a marked effect on responses and on the meaning of subgroup differences. When this is not recognized as a problem, however, it plays no specific role in the interpretation of findings.

In these introductory remarks I am trying to bring a set of issues to the surface by making problematic the "gap" between research interviewing and naturally occurring conversation. I have suggested that such technical procedures as coding and statistical analysis depend in a strong sense on the natural language competences of coders and investigators. This dependence is unexamined and therefore enters into interpretation in indirect and ad hoc ways. These procedures are characteristic of survey research interviewing, the dominant tradition of interview research in the social and behavioral sciences. Because survey research interviewing is modeled on the experimental method, which emphasizes standardized procedures, experimental control, quantitative measures, and statistical analysis, the role of language in coding and interpretation has remained implicit.

In later sections of this book, particularly in proposing an alternative approach, I shall have more to say about various forms of in-depth interviewing that differ in significant ways from survey interviews. It is not uncommon to view these other ways as "unscientific," as faulted departures from the ideal model. Restricting my critical examination of interview research, here and in the next chapter, primarily to survey interviewing reflects both the dominance of this tradition and the extent to which it tends to serve as the basis for assessing the merits of other approaches.[2]

My perspective, developed in the following chapters, is informed and shaped by a view of interviewing as a form of discourse between speakers. Questioning and answering are ways of speaking that are grounded in and depend on culturally shared and often tacit assumptions about how to express and understand beliefs, experiences, feelings, and intentions. I have referred to this knowledge as ordinary language competence. Proposing, as I have in this Introduction, that the ordinary language competence shared by investigators and respondents is a critical but unrecognized precondition for effective research practice is intended as a preliminary outline of this perspective and its implications.

In the mainstream tradition, the nature of interviewing as a form of discourse between speakers has been hidden from view by a dense screen of technical procedures. Disconnected from problems of meaning, problems that would necessarily remain at the forefront of investigative efforts if interviews were understood as discourse, techniques have taken on a life of their own. In this process attention has shifted radically away from the original purpose of interviewing as a research method, namely, to understand what respondents mean by what they say in response to our queries and thereby to arrive at a description of respondents' worlds of meaning that is adequate to the tasks of systematic analysis and theoretical interpretation.

My aim is to restore this original purpose to interviewing as a research method and to recover its distinctiveness and its special strengths as a method of inquiry in the human sciences. The first step, undertaken in the next chapter, is a reexamination of standard definitions of the research interview and of their assumptions and implications. This is my way of making interviewing problematic, of opening up the method to critical analysis. I will propose, and develop in successive chapters, an alternative definition that rests squarely on a concept of interviewing as a form of discourse.

1

Standard Practice

The way that our everyday, ordinary practice of asking and answering questions has been formalized into a research method is illustrated in standard definitions of interviewing found in textbooks and manuals. In this chapter, as background to developing an alternative approach, I examine the assumptions and implications of these definitions and focus on how the standard view of interviewing constrains research to "merely" technical issues and obscures the central problem of discourse.[1]

In a widely cited review, Maccoby and Maccoby (1954, p. 449) offer the following definition: "For our purposes, an interview will refer to a face-to-face verbal interchange, in which one person, the interviewer, attempts to elicit information or expressions of opinion or belief from another person or persons." A similar definition is found in Kahn and Cannell's (1957, p. 16) influential text: "We use the term interview to refer to a specialized pattern of verbal interaction—initiated for a specific purpose, and focused on some specific content area, with consequent elimination of extraneous material. Moreover, the interview is a pattern of interaction in which the role relationship of interviewer and respondent is highly specialized, its specific characteristics depending somewhat on the purpose and character of the interview."

Any assertion about uniformity of approach must be advanced with caution. Nonetheless these definitions appear to be widely accepted among investigators, as is evident from examination of studies based on interviews as well as of research on problems of interviewing, even when definitions either are more casual than those cited above or are left implicit. Schuman and Presser (1981, p. 1), for example, in reporting their studies of effects on responses of question wording and question order, do not provide a specific definition but refer in passing to the survey interview as combining sampling methods with "the ancient but extremely efficient method of obtaining information from people by asking questions." Sometimes the definition is even more oblique or indirect, as in Kidder's (1981) revision of a standard text on methods. Kidder makes little distinction between questionnaire and interview and notes that in both "heavy reliance is placed on verbal reports from the subjects for information about the stimuli or experiences to which they are exposed and for knowledge of their behavior" (p. 146). And sometimes a definition is omitted even where it might be expected, as in the *Interviewer's Manual* of the Survey Research Center (1976) at the University of Michigan, which includes extensive discussion of problems and much advice on how to conduct "them" but presents no explicit definition of interviews.

These instances of indirectness and implicitness presume that we all "know" what an interview is, at least if we are members of the research community, and that although there may still be technical problems interviewing is essentially nonproblematic as a method. Within this context of a taken-for-granted understanding, analyses and discussions of the interviewing method reveal the same assumptions that may more clearly be discerned in the explicit definitions cited earlier.

The first assumption is that an interview is a behavioral rather than a linguistic event. The definitions refer to an interview not as speech, or talk, or even communication, but as a "verbal exchange," a "pattern of verbal interaction," or a "verbal report." In this way the definitions erase and remove from consideration the primary and distinctive characteristic of an interview as discourse, that is, as meaningful speech between interviewer and interviewee as speakers of a shared language. The difference between a conception of interviewing as a form of talk and a concept "verbal interchange" or "verbal interaction" is far from trivial. It marks radically different understandings of the nature of the interview, of its special qualities, and of its problems.

Talk and behavior, as key alternative terms for conceptualizing interviews as well as other types of human action and experience, contrast with each other in highly significant ways.[2] Situations and forms of talk have structures—that is, forms of systematic organization—that reflect the operation of several types of normative rules—for example, rules of syntax, semantics, and pragmatics, to use a familiar scheme. As is true of other culturally grounded norms, these rules guide how individuals enter into situations, define and frame their sense of what is appropriate or inappropriate to say, and provide the basis for their understandings of what is said. This view of talk applies specifically in interviews, as we shall see later, to both interviewers' and respondents' understandings of the meaning and intent of questions and responses. Units of behavior, on the other hand, are arbitrary and fragmented and become connected and related to one another not through higher-order rules but through a history of past associations and reinforcements that varies from person to person. This view allows, and indeed encourages, interviewers and analysts to treat each question-answer pair as an isolated exchange.

The standard conception of interviewing as behavior, albeit verbal behavior, excludes explicit recognition of the cultural patterning of situationally relevant talk. The behavioral definition removes from consideration, in the analysis and interpretation of interviews, the normatively grounded and culturally shared understandings of interviews as particular types of speech situations. In turn, the consequent decontextualizing of questions and responses leads to a variety of problems in the analysis and interpretation of interview data. These problems are viewed as "technical," that is, as problems that can be "solved" through more precise and rigorous methods. They may usefully be thought of as research iatrogenic, generated by the behavioral approach itself rather than inherent in the interview. They result from the assumptions of the behavioral approach to interviewing, not from problems faced by all individuals in talking with and understanding one another. The problems include, for example, variation across interviewers, unreliability of coding, and the ambiguities and possible spuriousness of relationships among variables. Typical efforts to deal with them include, respectively, systematic interviewer training programs, elaborate coding manuals, and complex multivariate statistical analyses.

I am not mounting an argument against rigor and precision in research. Sophisticated, technical methods are integral to any scientific study. I am proposing, however, that the widespread view of interviews as behavioral events leads to the definition of certain problems as technical when the problem goes much deeper. Technical solutions are applied unreflectively, they become routine practice, and the presuppositions that underlie the approach remain unexamined. The sense of precision provided by these methods is illusory because they tend to obscure rather than illuminate the central problem in the interpretation of interviews, namely, the relationship between discourse and meaning.

One consequence of the behavioral approach is the almost total neglect by interview researchers of work by students of language on the rules, forms, and functions of questions and responses. There exists a respectable and instructive body of theoretical and empirical work on these topics by philosophers of language, linguists, sociolinguists, anthropologists, and sociologists. Dillon (1981), for example, recently compiled a preliminary bibliography of over two hundred articles on questioning as a form of speech, putting particular emphasis on studies in education and on the interactive functions of questions. His list includes only a handful of reports from the extensive literature in survey and opinion research, and in turn this literature, which focuses on different problems, rarely refers to work on questioning in linguistics and sociolinguistics.

Interest in this topic has grown over the past decade and a number of social scientists have explored linguistic and conversational rules that apply to questioning and answering in naturally occurring conversation. Goffman (1976), for example, examines linguistic and social constraints in conversation and the differences between replies and responses. Labov and Fanshel (1977) elaborate a formal set of rules for legitimate requests and their variants, with questions as one type of request. Mishler (1975a,b, 1978) shows systematic regularities in successive chains of questions and answers. Schegloff and Sacks (1973) and Sacks, Schegloff, and Jefferson (1974) develop the concept of adjacency pairs for the situation where a second speaker's utterances are tied to and contingent in particular ways to a first speaker's utterances, a conversational structure of which questions and answers are one important subtype. Briggs (1983, 1984) and Frake (1964, 1977) discuss the uses and problems of formal questioning procedures in ethnographic field research in other cultures.

This brief and noninclusive list is intended only to document the generalization made above that there is a serious and substantial tradition of theory and research on questions and answers, the central and distinctive feature of interviews, that is not represented in the dominant approach to interview research. Except for the few reports on survey research noted by each of them, there is an almost total lack of overlap between Dillon's (1981) bibliography and the extensive bibliographies included in recent books summarizing studies of questions and answers in survey interviews by Dijkstra and van der Zouwen (1982) and by Schuman and Presser (1981). The relatively total neglect of linguistically oriented theoretical and empirical work on questions and answers by investigators in the survey research tradition directly reflects the definition adopted by the latter of the interview as a behavioral event, as a verbal interchange, rather than as a speech event—that is, as discourse.

A second assumption of the standard approach in interview research, closely linked to its behavioral bias, is its reliance on the stimulus-response paradigm of the experimental laboratory for conceptualization of the interview process and, consequently, for specification of issues for research. Brenner (1982, p. 131) explicitly invokes this model as a research framework in his review of studies of the "role" of interviewers and the "rules" of interviewing: "It is useful, if only heuristically, to think of the question-answer process in the survey interview in stimulus-response terms . . . The stimulus-response analogy is useful because the only objective of survey interviewing consists in obtaining respondents' verbal reactions to the questions put to them, these meeting particular response requirements posed by the questions." By specifying the objective as obtaining "verbal reactions," Brenner makes explicit the connection between the stimulus-response model of interviewing and the behavioristic assumption. Brenner then draws implications from this analogy:

> Attempts to implement the stimulus-response analogy, in as much as is possible, require, first the standardization of the questionnaire to be used in the interviews. In order to maximize the effect of the questions qua stimuli, it is also necessary to try to ensure that the interviewing techniques used do not affect the answering process other than in terms of facilitating the accomplishment of, in measurement terms, adequate responses—that is, answers which are contingent upon the questions alone . . . Also, in order to achieve reliability and precision in the ways in which interviews are conducted (both are prerequisites for assuming the equivalence of interviews in terms of interviewer-respondent interaction), the interviewing techniques must be determined, and standardized, before the data collection commences.   (pp. 131–132)

By and large, research on problems of the interview has been framed within the stimulus-response paradigm, implicit reliance on its assumptions guiding the general direction of inquiry and generating the specific questions for study. The primary aim of this research and of recommendations for practice based on it is to ensure, in accord with Brenner's prescription, the "equivalence of interviews in terms of interviewer-respondent interaction." Because the "stimulus" is a compound one, consisting in interviewer plus question, it is not surprising to find the majority of studies directed to two general questions: How are respondents' answers influenced by the form and wording of questions? and How are they influenced by interviewer characteristics?

The intent of these studies is to find ways to standardize the stimulus or, perhaps a better term, to neutralize it, so that responses may be interpreted clearly and unequivocally. That is, the aim is to ascertain respondents' "true" opinions and to minimize possible distortions and biases in responses that may result from question or interviewer variables that interfere with respondents' abilities or wishes to express their "real" or "true" views. Such potentially confounding variables include, for example, whether a question is phrased in negative or positive terms, the number and placement of alternative response categories, the sequential order of questions, and particular social attributes, expectations, or attitudes of interviewers.

Dijkstra and van der Zouwen (1982, p. 3), who refer to this as the general problem of "response effects," note that the central concern of interview research is with "distortions because of the effects of improper variables, that is, variables other than the respondent's opinion, etc. that the researcher is interested in." In a similar vein Hagenaars and Heinen (1982, p. 92), reviewing studies of the effects on responses of selected interviewer social characteristics, state that "the main feature of the registered response that will be of interest is response bias: the difference between the registered score and the true score."

This is not the place to detail the findings of a large number of studies; several recent reviews serve this purpose, for example, Cannell, Miller, and Oksenberg (1981), the papers in Dijkstra and van der Zouwen (1982), and the monograph by Schuman and Presser (1981). However, it is germane to my argument to assess in broad terms the net result of this line of investigative effort. The following generalization is warranted, I believe, as a statement of the level of understanding that has been achieved regarding the effects of interviewer and question variables: some variables, and perhaps all of them, have some effects on some, and perhaps all, types of response under some conditions. Or, restated in somewhat different terms: each stimulus variable studied may influence some feature(s) of a response, the magnitude and seriousness of the effect being a function of various contextual factors.

This is a disturbing conclusion, all the more so because such a statement could have been made prior to undertaking the studies. Further, the conclusion and the findings that it reflects have no practical implications for the design of any particular study because the possible relationships between stimulus and response variables have to be determined separately in each instance.

I am aware that this is a harsh and sweeping generalization. It may be mitigated to some extent by the observation that many investigators arrive at a similar conclusion, although they often place it in the more positive context of the evident need for future research. This mixture of criticism and hopefulness is expressed clearly by Presser (1983) in his recent essay review of three books on survey research methodology and practice, including the Dijkstra and van der Zouwen (1982) collection cited here. Presser, coauthor of another major study (Schuman and Presser, 1981), retains a more optimistic view than I do about the potential value of survey research, but his comments are in full agreement with the argument I have advanced here.

> It is striking, though, how little influenced most survey practice is by this accumulated knowledge. The typical survey is conducted in ignorance or disregard of methodological findings . . . To begin with, methodological research sometimes produces conflicting findings or findings difficult to interpret. This is true, for instance, of studies of the differences between agree-disagree and forced-choice question formats . . . In many other areas, data-collection issues have not been subjected to much systematic inquiry . . . Finally, methodological research sometimes produces results that have no clear implication for practice . . . meaning . . . is affected by the order of the questions . . . as with many other demonstrations of context effects, it points to the importance of contexts, but not to any practical guide for ordering survey items. (pp. 637–638)

Beza (1984), in an essay review of three different books reporting findings of within-survey experiments on such problems as question order and question form, including the Schuman and Presser (1981) study discussed below, arrives at a conclusion that echoes my own and Presser's about the limited value of such studies for research practice: "Perhaps the most important conclusion to be drawn from the three books is that the answers to questions often depend on question form and respondent understanding. Consequently, investigators interested in assessing the impact of question form and respondent understanding need to conduct their own experiments within surveys" (p. 37).

Given the extent and seriousness of these problems—the ambiguity and often contradictory nature of findings from methodological studies and the lack of any general guidelines that would apply across different studies—we can more easily understand why research reports and review essays are pervaded by "on the one hand, on the other hand" locutions, why caution is expressed about drawing firm conclusions or overgeneralizing from the data, and why interpretations are wrapped in layers of qualifications. Thus, DeLamater (1982), summarizing findings on the effects of variations in the wording of questions directed to the same topic, remarks: "It may be incorrect to think that it is possible to have alternative wordings of the 'same' item. Any change in wording can change the meaning of the question. Whether two items are equivalent should be treated as a question to be answered analytically, using techniques such as interitem correlations, factor analyses, and analyses which focus on substantive relationships involving each item" (p. 23). Noting the absence of "systematic" effects, that is, general effects that hold across surveys and content areas, he points to the significance of contextual relationships: "The available research does not find systematic effects of either interviewer or respondent characteristics. When such person variables are related to responses, it is primarily in interaction with particular types of questions or characteristics of the data collection situation" (p. 38).

Molenaar (1982) concludes in a similar vein regarding variation in question wording: "Moreover, hardly any experiment gives a decisive answer as to which of the question-wordings involved is more valid. Thus, also the direct practical utility of any generalizing statement may be said to be fairly restricted, in that it does not constitute practical guidelines for framing questions" (p. 51). Reviewing the effects of differences in the form of response alternatives, Molenaar asserts: "The effects, however, will vary with the content of the questions and with the nature of the added contrasting alternative(s)." Similarly, with regard to the effects of directive as compared with nondirective questions, he states: "the effects of directive question-forms on the responses, . . . seem to be dependent for example, on characteristics of the respondents, the content and the context of the question concerned" (p. 70).

These citations could easily be multiplied, but it may be more useful to consider in some detail a particular example of a topic regarding which "data collection issues have not been subjected to much systematic inquiry" (Presser, 1983, p. 637). Brenner (1982) conducted one of the few studies that directly examines, through the analysis of tape-recorded interviews, whether interviewers actually ask the questions on the interview schedule. Exact questioning is central to the basic requirement within the stimulus-response paradigm of a standard stimulus for all respondents. He finds that "only roughly two-thirds of all questions were asked as required. Thus, in all, it is clear, for this survey, that respondents were frequently not presented with equivalent stimuli" (p. 150).

Brenner's high percentage of nonequivalence is similar to levels reported in three other studies. Bradburn and Sudman (1979) found that more than one-third of the questions in their survey were altered by interviewers. Cannell, Lawson, and Hausser (1975) classified interviewer behaviors into a variety of categories as acceptable or unacceptable with regard to the relative degree of "correctness" in questions asked, meaning in what ways interviewers deviated from the question printed in the interview schedule and whether these deviations altered the meaning of the question. They report, "approximately three-quarters of the activity was acceptable, and a sizeable 25% was judged to be unacceptable" (p. 85). These authors also report an earlier study of their own in which "tape recordings showed that 36% of the questions were not asked as written and 20% were altered sufficiently to destroy comparability" (p. 4). Both Brenner and Cannell and co-workers also find a high degree of variation among interviewers, and the latter group also reports considerable variation across interviews conducted by the same interviewers. Finally, in a particularly well designed field experiment that focused on the "adequacy" of interviewers' questions, that is, on whether interviewers altered "the essential content or meaning of the text" (p. 44), Dijkstra, van der Veen, and van der Zouwen (1985) found "at least one such inadequate interviewer action" in 40 percent of the question-answer exchanges. "In other words, in 40% of all Q-A sequences, the information obtained cannot be trusted, because of the occurrence of interviewer actions that may have biased the responses" (p. 60).

Brenner (1982, p. 163) concludes that his findings paint a "somewhat alarming picture . . . This implies that much of scientific survey research involves practices of data collection which are at variance with the quest for measurement to which survey researchers commonly subscribe." In making this judgment, he qualifies it by noting the difficulty of generalizing his results, that is, of determining how representative his findings are. "Given the complete absence of detailed studies of interviewer-respondent interaction in routine survey research, it is, of course, impossible to answer this question."

These studies are based on the performance of experienced and well-trained interviewers in carefully designed studies under the direction of competent investigators. We do not know how typical these levels of "incorrectness" and variation among interviewers are in "routine survey research," but it is not unlikely that the problem would be more serious in studies that rely on interviewers who are less carefully trained and supervised. Brenner's conclusion is compatible with the sweeping generalization I stated earlier. One cannot expect strong and consistent findings if the basic data-collection procedure, the survey interview itself, is so unreliable and uncertain.

Brenner's qualification about his "somewhat alarming picture" is even more alarming in its implications when we realize that it reflects the relatively total absence of studies of interviewer performance. With the exception of rare "field experiments" like those noted above, the key assumption of the stimulus-response paradigm—that the questions asked are standardized and represent the "same" stimulus for all respondents—is almost never examined in actual studies.

The results are no more encouraging to confidence in the survey interview as a method when we turn to features that have been studied. Molenaar (1982, pp. 81–82), for example, in his review cited earlier of studies of the "formal" characteristics of questions, concludes that with regard to "wording variations": "It seems that nearly every type does have effects to some degree . . . the available data indicate that the effects (or related phenomena) of some wording-variables tend to be fairly systematic (although the variation in the data is quite large); the effects of some other variables seem to be as yet rather conditioned and less straightforward . . . Whether the effects are systematic or not, the basic fact is that wording-effects do occur on a large scale." His conclusion, with the vague and indeterminate phrasings "it seems that," "to some degree," "seem to be as yet," reaffirms the general assertion with which I began this section, namely, that some variables, and perhaps all of them, have some effects on some, and perhaps all, types of response under some conditions.

The reason that Molenaar and other reviewers find it difficult to arrive at firmer and less vague conclusions can be more fully understood and appreciated if we examine the findings of a particular study. Schuman and Presser's (1981) monograph is a useful and instructive source of guidance for addressing this problem. Their series of studies of question wording and question order are elegant and extensive, and they are judicious and cautious in their observations and conclusions about their work and that of others. Their report has already been hailed as a "classic text" and as "exemplary" (Beza, 1984, p. 35). They begin by noting the decline of interest in the effects on responses of how questions are worded: "By the early 1950s such question-wording experiments had largely disappeared from major surveys . . . Our present research returns to the question-wording experiments of four decades ago" (pp. 4–5).[3]

With regard to question-order effects, Schuman and Presser (1981) remark that they did not initially believe that these effects would be important and they end believing that they are not pervasive. "But they are clearly more common, greater in magnitude, and more varied in direction than we had thought, and they constitute a serious problem for surveys and an important complication to our own research" (p. 306). Referring in general to the problem of context effects—how the sequencing of questions and responses influences answers to individual items—they state that "it is necessary only to indicate the likelihood that some of our methodological results are contingent on context in ways that are not visible or are visible only in the form of contradictory findings. The whole effort to generalize about question form must usually pretend that each question can be viewed in isolation, but of course this is incorrect" (p. 308). And they proceed with a qualification that is by now a familiar one to readers of this book, by observing that the findings presented on question wording throughout their book "depend in often unknown ways" (p. 309) on context effects. Finally, they refer the difficulties of research on these topics to the inherent problem of language and meaning: "Last, but hardly least, is the fact that language is not a set of formal classes or boxes, but . . . a medium in which we exist . . . Thus every attempt to design experiments that deal with generic question forms flies in the face of the fact that every question is unique. Experiments on form seek to draw generalizations from a material that resists generalization, that is particular and plastic and seamless. This may well be the greatest obstacle of all" (pp. 310–311).

These observations about language and the uniqueness of each question are fully consonant with the critique developed here of the stimulus-response model and of other assumptions of the standard approach to interviewing. Unfortunately, Schuman and Presser arrive at this position only at the end of their research; their work is not informed by this understanding. Further, their recommendations for survey practice and additional studies remain bound within the traditional model.

This review of research on response effects makes it clear that the idea of a standard stimulus is chimerical and that the quest for "equivalence of interviews in terms of interviewer-respondent interaction" is misdirected and bound to fail. The question-answer format guides and organizes the discourse of interviewers and respondents, but they are talking together, not "behaving" as stimulus-senders and response-emitters. It is their general competence as language users and not simply interviewing "skills" or techniques that underlies their abilities to engage in this type of talk.

Lazarsfeld (1935), one of the great pioneers of survey research, understood that variability in how interviewers ask questions is the key to good interviewing and not a problem to be solved by standardization. He recommends a different approach than appears to have been adopted by successive generations of researchers. He refers to the "principle of division," the aim of which is to adapt "the pattern of our questionnaire to the structural pattern of the experience of the respondent" (p. 4). He recognized that the attempt to fit questions to respondents' different experiences was, even then, in conflict with usual procedure and traditional opinion for questions to be worded in the same way for all respondents. Instead, he argues, "we advocate a rather loose and liberal handling of a questionnaire by an interviewer. It seems to us much more important that the question be fixed in its meaning, than in the wording" (p. 4). Of course, to follow this principle would require tape-recording interviews so that the "meanings" of the questions asked by different interviewers could be determined; as we have seen, such studies are rare.

In addition to the behavioral bias and the stimulus-response model discussed above, two other assumptions of the traditional approach to the interview merit separate comment. The first is suggested by Schuman and Presser's observation, cited earlier, that attempts to generalize about question form "must usually pretend that each question can be viewed in isolation." They are concerned with the contextual effects of question order, but the problem of context is a more general one. Survey research is a context-stripping procedure, and investigators "pretend" that a variety of contexts that affect the interview process and the meaning of questions and answers are not present.[4]

As they strip away the structure and flow of the full interview as a context for understanding each question-answer exchange, researchers tend also to isolate the interview situation as a whole from both broad cultural and local subcultural norms and frameworks of meaning. Riesman and Benney (1955, 1956), directors of the early and now rarely cited Interview Project at the University of Chicago, make the acute observation that the spread of interviewing is dependent on the spread of the "modern temper." They suggest that interviewing requires the development of a culture with a high degree of individuation between persons and differentiation within society and argue that it would not be possible "if we did not have well-established conventions governing the meeting of strangers" (1956, p. 229).

Benney and Hughes (1956), noting that "the interview is a relatively new kind of encounter in the history of human relations" (p. 193), assert: "Where languages are too diverse, where common values are too few, where the fear of talking to strangers is too great, there the interview based on a standardized questionnaire calling for a few standardized answers may not be applicable. Those who venture into such situations may have to invent new modes of interviewing" (p. 191). These insights appear to have been forgotten as interviewing has become a routine technical practice and a pervasive, taken-for-granted activity in our culture. That is, rather than inventing "new modes of interviewing" specifically designed for each of the diverse contexts and subcultures of a complex society, mainstream researchers rigidly apply a standard method as if it had universal cross-cultural and transhistorical validity. This is another instance that marks how the essentially problematic nature of interviewing as a tool of inquiry is obscured by an emphasis on it as a technical practice.[5]

The problem raised by so radical a decontextualization of the interview at so many different levels is deeper than the technical methodological one of whether the answer to a prior question influences answers to next questions. The more significant problem is that respondents' answers are disconnected from essential sociocultural grounds of meaning. Each answer is a fragment removed both from its setting in the organized discourse of the interview and from the life setting of the respondent. Answers can be understood, or at least interpreted by the investigator, only by reintroducing these contexts through a variety of presuppositions and assumptions, and this is usually done implicitly and in an ad hoc fashion. I have already alluded in the Introduction to how this occurs at the step of coding.

Cicourel's (1982) comments reflect a critical perspective similar to the one developed here. He discusses a number of cultural, linguistic, and psychlogical presuppositions of survey research and, addressing the particular contextual problem of the ecological validity of interviews, asks, "Do our instruments capture the daily life conditions, opinions, values, attitudes, and knowledge base of those we study as expressed in their natural habitat?" (p. 15). More specifically, what is "the extent to which responses to interview and survey questions reflect or represent the daily actions of a collectivity" (p. 16)? In an earlier paper, using case examples of families that he came to know through extended periods of observation and interaction, Cicourel (1967) argues that investigators must "seek to understand the respondent's utterances as employed and intended by the users within the socially organized context of the family interviewed, and the relationship of the interviewer and respondent" (p. 78). Without an understanding of family organization, the researcher has no "contextual basis for interpreting responses to particular questions that may or may not touch areas relevant to the respondent's life circumstances" (p. 79).

Cicourel's point, of course, has a range of implication extending well beyond the family as a context for understanding respondents' answers. The one-shot interview conducted by an interviewer without local knowledge of a respondent's life situation and following a standard schedule that explicitly excludes attention to particular circumstances—in short, a meeting between strangers unfamiliar with each other's "socially organized contexts" of meaning—does not provide the necessary contextual basis for adequate interpretation. The attempted solution to this problem is reliance on sampling and associated procedures of statistical analysis; this approach undergirds survey research. The set of assumptions embodied in statistical analysis reinforce the standard model of interviewing. Although I have focused primarily on interviewing as a field procedure and pointed to problems of data interpretation that are a consequence of the stimulus-response paradigm, it is clear that these assumptions are intertwined with the requirements for statistical analysis of data. The latter reflect back on and shape the form and objectives of interviews.

Earlier I cited Schuman's (1982, p. 22) observation that the origin of surveys lies in two intellectual inclinations, the first to ask questions and the second "to draw samples to represent a much larger universe." The wish to generalize is implemented by sampling procedures for selecting respondents and statistical methods for assessing the limits within which findings based on samples can be generalized to larger populations. The importance of this approach is evident in the tables and statistical tests around which research reports are organized and in the array of complex methods of multivariate analysis. Less evident is the overall impact of this approach on how the interview itself is conceived and conducted, a point noted many years ago by Benney and Hughes (1956): "However vaguely this is conceived by the actual participants, it is the needs of the statistician rather than of the people involved directly that determine much, not only [of] the content of communication but its form as well . . . At its most obvious the convention of comparability produces the 'standardized' interview . . . and little freedom is permitted the interviewer to adjust the statisticians' needs to the particular encounter" (p. 141).

An extended critique of reliance on quantitative data and statistical methods is beyond the scope and intent of this book, and it is certainly not unique to survey research. Here it must suffice to note that Benney and Hughes's observation points to the internal consistency of the several assumptions of the dominant approach to interviewing. At the end stage of a study, statistical criteria provide the "meaning" of findings and guide interpretation and directions of theorizing. Investigators search for "patterns" in the responses of different subpopulations by making comparisons between groups of respondents differing in one or a combination of sociodemographic characteristics, such as age, gender, income, and education. Cicourel (1982, pp. 19–20) points to the general problem of this approach to interpretation: "The primary difficulty remains the absence of strong theories. Instead of using strong theories we invariably rely on the detection of patterning in survey responses in order to guide us in making theoretical explanations after the fact. Theory seldom guides social research explicitly; we depend on research findings to decide which theoretical concepts seem appropriate."

One reason for the lack of strong theories is that the respondent groupings that serve as the units of analysis are not real social or individual entities. That is, the basic data are distributions or summary scores aggregated across separate responses of individual respondents. We have already seen that each response is a fragment removed from the psychological and social contexts of the respondent as well as from the full discourse of the interview. When these responses are assembled into different subgroups, by age, gender, and the like, the results are artificial aggregates that have no direct representation in the real world of communities, social institutions, families, or persons. The incommensurability between these real social units of action and meaning and the artificial aggregates about which survey researchers "theorize" is one of the principal reasons that theories are necessarily weak, based on ad hoc rather than systematic hypotheses, and saturated with a variety of implicit presuppositions.

Other Critical Views of the Survey Interview: A Comparison

This critique of the currently dominant approach to interviewing as a research method began with the observation of a gap between asking and answering in naturally occurring, contextually grounded conversations and the question-response process in standard interviews. I noted the paradox that although this problem rarely receives explicit attention, many of the techniques and procedures used routinely in interview research represent efforts to mitigate the consequences of this gap. For example, to minimize effects of unavoidable variations in interview contexts, investigators try to standardize interviewers, questions, and responses.

The thrust of my argument is that these efforts have failed and, further, that the failure may be traced to a set of assumptions underlying the standard approach that are inconsistent with the essential feature of interviewing as organized social discourse. By adopting an approach that is behavioral and antilinguistic, relies on the stimulus-response model, and decontextualizes the meaning of responses, researchers have attempted to avoid rather than to confront directly the interrelated problems of context, discourse, and meaning. Put somewhat differently, standard practice provides a set of blinders that excludes this set of problems from a researcher's field of vision. Work is done as if they did not exist, and the work goes forward. Unfortunately, wishing does not make it so, and the social reality that remains alive and active outside this restricted field of vision continues to exert its effects.

Although the survey interview is the dominant methodological paradigm for interview research in the social and behavioral sciences, it has not gone unchallenged. My assessment of its limitations would be shared, at least in part, by many other critics.[6] Some of the most severe critics come from within the ranks of survey researchers. Nonetheless, much of this criticism has tended to take the form of a salvage operation, the aim being to "save" the survey interview despite its defects. I will not attempt to review this literature, but it may be useful at this point to take note of some representative examples of other critical views and, by contrast, clarify and make more explicit the perspective adopted here.

In the eclectic manner typical of authors of introductory texts on methods, Lofland (1971) devotes a chapter to the "unstructured interview." Because he views this approach in a positive light, his remarks regarding how it contrasts with the structured interview are particularly instructive. He states that the structured interview is a "legitimate strategy" when the investigator knows "what the important questions are and, more importantly, what the main kinds of answers can be" (p. 75). In contrast, the unstructured interview is characterized as a "flexible strategy of discovery . . . Its object is to carry on a guided conversation and to elicit rich, detailed materials that can be used in qualitative analysis" (p. 76). Reviewing a number of studies based on this approach, in addition to suggesting guidelines for un-structured interviewing, he observes that it is "a research strat-egy of some reasonably frequent use and significance in generating social scientific description and analysis" (p. 76).

I find the contrast somewhat invidious and all the more no-table in that respect because it comes from a friend of relatively open-ended field methods. The terms of his discussion imply that if a researcher is knowledgeable and has thought clearly about the problem under study, she or he will choose the struc-tured interview as the preferred strategy. On the other hand, the less knowledgeable investigator who is unclear about the topic and aims of the study can turn to the "flexible strategy of discovery," namely, the unstructured interview.

Some investigators who adopt the unstructured interview as a deliberate alternative to the standard approach qualify their work as preliminary or exploratory; their guarded descriptions of the method tend to undermine the argument for its use. For example Luker (1975), in her study of contraceptive risk taking among women seeking an abortion, explicitly rejects structured interviews in favor of unstructured interviews and an interpre-tive procedure referred to by Glaser and Strauss (1967) as "grounded theory." She reports turning to the latter as a type of "hypothesis-generating" study when it became clear that the requisite assumptions of the standard survey design and inter-view could not be met: "The conclusions seemed inescapable. There were no readily agreed-upon hypotheses to be tested, there were not sufficient resources to test such hypotheses even if they did exist, and even if resources to test such hypotheses had been available, widespread access was not. As a result, hy-pothesis testing of the kind generally envisioned in survey re-search was out of the question" (p. 158).

Luker describes how this approach allowed her to develop and test hypotheses and to construct a "heuristic model that closely approximated classical decision-making theory" (p. 165). In the end, however, her initial qualifications about the method, reflected in her references to her work as an "explor-atory study" and a "preliminary investigation" (p. 158), extend to her assessment of the import and significance of her findings: "Although this is a preliminary study and the model which grew from it is still in the exploratory stage, further work can and should be done to extend it into a larger range of populations. [This extension] . . . should make the model useful in examining the larger problem of unwanted pregnancies in general" (p. 169).

In later chapters I shall be citing the work of other investigators who are more fully and directly committed to alternative approaches, but it is important to recognize from the beginning that the reservations expressed by Lofland and Luker represent the central and most prominent position on the relative adequacy and the merits of different methods. Alternatives to the standard approach, like unstructured interviewing, tend to be viewed as faulted variants. The implications of this position are that, given a well-thought-out research plan, specific hypotheses, and sufficient resources, the structured interview is the preferred choice. The position I have adopted here and will be developing throughout this book counters this view. I am arguing, instead, that the standard survey interview is itself essentially faulted and that it therefore cannot serve as the ideal methodological model against which to assess other approaches.

How researchers tend to address particular problems of interviewing suggests a further way that my critique differs from others. Among these problems, the relationship between interviewer and respondent has been a central topic. Although they are of equal significance in my perspective, I have by focusing primarily on the gap between naturally occurring conversations and interviews left these issues relatively implicit. Typically, they are framed as problems of rapport. Attention is directed to how an interviewer can establish a relationship that is conducive to a respondent's expression of beliefs and attitudes, given the special features of the interview situation. Interviewers are instructed in the "proper" role to adopt to maintain the cooperativeness of respondents. Lofland (1971), referring to his recommendations as the "conventional wisdom," states that "for most interviewing situations it is most productive of information for the interviewer to assume a non-argumentative, supportive, and sympathetically understanding attitude" (p. 89). Noting the potential hazards of a different stance, he goes on, "I would say that successful interviewing is not unlike carrying on unthreatening, self-controlled, supportive, polite, and cordial interaction in everyday life" (p. 90).

Other commentators make a sharper distinction between ordinary, everyday relationships and the requirements of an interview. The former are viewed as governed by social norms that depend on trust, mutuality, and openness to the potential for intimacy that comes with shared disclosure of beliefs and values. Standard interviews are more asymmetric and hierarchical. For example, interviewers initiate topics, direct the flow of talk, decide when a response is adequate, and only interviewees disclose their views. To establish and maintain rapport in this special and nonordinary situation, interviewers must rely on what may be called "mock" representations of the features of ordinary relationships. Riessman (1977, p. 33), reviewing the literature on role relationships in interviews, observes that "confounding" personal qualities of everyday social relationships with those required of an interviewer may obscure how data reflect the special nature of the interview situation: "As the majority of data in the social sciences are gathered via this procedure, one needs to be aware of the unique aspects of this two person interaction and potential effects on the validity on the data obtained. Although free from the artificiality of the laboratory . . . the survey interview also is not free of artificiality and contrivance. Moreover, the very ways in which it is atypical of other two person interactions pinpoint the portals through which invalidity can creep."

Recognizing these problems, Riessman nonetheless directs her efforts to their management and control. Oakley (1981) mounts an attack on the "conventional wisdom" and the standard approach to interviewing that resonates closely with my own position. She is concerned with the broad issue of a feminist approach to research in contrast to the dominant "masculine" model and begins, as she puts it in her title, with the "contradiction in terms" of a feminist interviewing women. She notes that, although much of modern sociology depends on data gathered through interviewing, "very few sociologists who employ interview data actually bother to describe in detail the process of interviewing itself" (p. 31). Further, the criterion as to what is legitimate or illegitimate to include in a research report reflects a masculine model of research and "has led to an unreal theoretical characterization of the interview as a means of gathering sociological data which cannot and does not work in practice" (p. 31).

In a wide-ranging critique of the "hygienic" "textbook paradigm" of research interviewing, Oakley observes that "what is good for interviewers is not necessarily good for interviewees" (p. 40). She argues that the emphasis in standard practice on objectivity, detachment, and the hierarchical relationship between interviewer and interviewee is "morally indefensible" and has "general and irreconcilable contradictions" at its heart (p. 41). Noting the requirement for neutrality and the assumption in methods manuals that the goal of perfection in interviewing can be attained, she asserts that "the contradiction between the need for 'rapport' and the requirement of between interview comparability cannot be solved" (p. 51). She proposes a mode of interviewing that requires personal responsiveness and involvement on the part of the interviewer. Her conclusion has general import as well as specific relevance to this discussion. "A feminist methodology . . . requires, further, that the mythology of 'hygienic' research with its accompanying mystification of the researcher and the researched as objective instruments of data production be replaced by the recognition that personal involvement is more than dangerous bias—it is the condition under which people come to know each other and to admit others into their lives" (p. 58).

I shall have more to say about these issues in Chapter 5, in a discussion of studies that seek to empower respondents. For the moment, Oakley's work serves to alert us to the deeper significance of the "conventional wisdom" by pointing to how standard requirements for "neutrality" and "rapport" may at the same time both conceal and incorporate the pervasive hierarchical structure of relationships in society. It is another example of how the dominant concern with technical issues obscures more fundamental questions about research practice.

Although, as Luker's comments cited earlier suggest, the survey design and interview is often viewed as a type of hypothesis-testing study, I have already noted that statistical findings tend to lead theory rather than the other way around. Veroff (1983) provides a well-worked-out and relatively elegant example of this relation between findings and theory in the course of an effort to resolve conflicting and contradictory findings. This is clearly an instance of a "salvage operation." Veroff attempts to explain, that is, to develop a theory that would account for, the sometimes inconsistent findings between two national, comparable surveys conducted twenty years apart to obtain "assessments of people's well-being, self-conceptions, reactions to life roles, and . . . the strength of their motives for achievement, affiliation, and power" (p. 333). He records the investigators' discovery of a problem: "Not until we discovered that motive-behavior connections varied across the 2 surveys or across different age and status groups did we become fully aware of the differential effect various contexts might have on personality characteristics" (p. 333). He recommends, given such findings, that personality be viewed "as dependent on a variety of contexts: historical, cultural (subcultural), developmental, organizational, and interpersonal" (p. 334).

Veroff uses this notion of context to interpret anomalous results. One example that illustrates his approach is the way he interprets an unexpected reversal of findings between two surveys. In 1957, the researchers found that "the higher the achievement motive, the more men expressed dissatisfaction with their work." Twenty years later, they found instead that "the stronger the achievement motive, the greater the job satisfaction" (p. 334). Veroff tries to account for this reversal by suggesting possible changes in or variations in each of the contexts. For example, with reference to the context of historical change, he suggests three alternative lines of interpretation. First, "the meaning of work or the meaning of the achievement motive, or both, were different in the two periods . . . Thus, to express job dissatisfactions may have had a different meaning to highly motivated persons in each period." Second, "the nature of men's achievement motive may have shifted from 1957 to 1976 . . . from the emphasis on task accomplishment in 1957 to an emphasis on the process of personal actualization by 1976." And third, because the scoring system for motives is based on "validation studies begun in the late 1940s, the criteria in coding may be historically biased . . . This kind of speculation raises the methodologically burdensome necessity of making different criteria for assessment of personality for different historical eras" (pp. 334–335).

Veroff's range of possible explanations is quite wide. The main point, however, is not whether one or all of the above is correct, but rather that the validity of each survey's findings is taken for granted; otherwise why bother to explain the reversal? Excluded from his initial list of contexts is the research context itself. All the features of interviewing discussed in this chapter and shown to be problematic are omitted from his discussion. His approach is, in this respect, representative of other survey researchers' efforts to interpret findings; theory is brought in at the end to explain inconsistencies or unexpected findings, which abound in all studies. Analyses of the interview process and of relations between language and meaning are neglected. As Oakley remarks, in the passage cited earlier, "few sociologists . . . bother to describe in detail the process of interviewing itself."

Despite the detail of exposition, the critique of the mainstream approach to interviewing presented here is preliminary to the main work of this book. Given the dominance of the survey interview model, it is necessary to document the frailty of the evidence in support of its assumptions. It is not my task to suggest ways it might be useful, despite its faults, for certain limited and specified purposes; there are many others to argue its case.[7] Rather, my central task is to develop an alternative that is more appropriate and more adequate for research in the human sciences. A new definition of interviewing is proposed and developed in the following chapters that in every respect counters the assumptions of the standard approach. It centers on a view of the interview as a discourse between speakers and on the ways that the meanings of questions and responses are contextually grounded and jointly constructed by interviewer and respondent. Successive chapters explicate the core components of this definition and its implications for research practice.

2

Research Interviews
as Speech Events

The concept of a speech event that I employ here is borrowed from Hymes (1967, p. 19), who used the term for "activities, or aspects of activities, that are directly governed by rules for the use of speech." Hymes is concerned with developing a taxonomy of social units that provides a comprehensive sociolinguistic description of the varieties of talk that take place in communities (see also Hymes, 1972 and 1981). Speech events represent one level in the hierarchy of such units that he specifies, among which are speech communities, speech situations, and speech acts. Gumperz's (1982) term *speech activities* might serve just as well in reformulating our thinking about the nature of interviews. In addition, and closely related to the view developed here, Gumperz emphasizes the emergence of meaning through interaction in his definition of a speech activity as "a set of social relationships enacted about a set of schemata in relation to some communicative goal." Different speech activities, such as chatting, telling a story, lecturing, and of course interviewing, "imply certain expectancies about thematic progression, turn taking rules, form, and outcome of the interaction as well as constraints on context" (p. 166). Defining interviews as speech events or speech activities, as I do, marks the fundamental contrast between the standard antilinguistic, stimulus-response model and an alternative approach to interviewing as discourse between speakers. Different definitions in and of themselves do not constitute different practices. Nonetheless, this new definition alerts us to features of interviews that hitherto have been neglected.[1]

For example, if the analysis of speech is central to the use of interviews as research data, then an accurate record is needed of the questions that interviewers ask and the responses that interviewees give. This seems obvious enough, yet the near-universal assumption and its accompanying practice in the mainstream approach is that the question is adequately represented by its formal statement in the text of an interview schedule and the answer by an interviewer's highly selective version of what a respondent said, usually in the form of on-the-spot written notes. It will be evident from work reported below that these procedures do not and cannot, because of the nature of interviews as discourse, produce a valid description of questions and responses. The governing assumptions of the standard approach are not empirically grounded, are of questionable validity, and are misleading guides to interpretation. Further, the problem of adequate representation emerges only when we take speech seriously, and this is the first significant consequence of redefining interviews as speech events.

We may begin to appreciate the nature and dimensions of the problem by examining typescripts of tape-recorded interviews. Excerpts from four interviews of two married couples conducted by me and Anita L. Mishler (1976) are presented in Transcript 1.[2] These separate interviews of husbands and wives took place about a week after a jointly conducted interview in which we both interviewed each of the two couples together. This work was part of a pilot study of the marriage and family history and current experiences of middle-aged couples who had recently become grandparents.

These interviews were conducted in 1976. The transcripts that appear here are reproduced from "typescripts" revised by me in 1982. Interviewers are labeled "E" and "A" for Elliot G. Mishler and Anita L. Mishler, respectively; the respondents are referred to as "H" for husbands and "W" for wives for the two couples, ML901 and ML902. In the transcripts notation is used to indicate certain features of speech: nonlexical expressions such as "Hm hm" and "A:ah"; interruptions and overlaps between speakers by a left-hand bracket "["; hesitations and pauses by "(P)." False starts and repetitions of words are preserved and unclear speech is enclosed in parentheses. One widely used system of typescript notation is presented in Jefferson (1978a), and a discussion of issues and problems of typescript preparation and of different approaches may be found in Mishler (1984, chap. 2).

The "question as text" preceding the excerpts comes directly from the interview schedule. It was designed to open the follow-up interview and to serve several purposes: to make a transition from the earlier joint interview, to reestablish the focus of interest of the study, to discover if there were any significant topics that had not emerged in the first interview or if the respondent had further thoughts about topics that had been discussed, to determine if there were any negative feelings or untoward consequences from the first interview, and to provide a general and open-ended framework for more specific structured questions in later sections of the interview schedule. Clearly, this is a heavy burden for one question to carry, as is reflected in the complexity of the question. The question as text offers a number of topics among which we might expect interviewers and respondents to vary in what they might select or emphasize, for example, further thoughts about *any* events, experiences, or feelings; significant "anythings" contemplated since the last interview; important changes occurring at any time in their lives.

One feature of the introductory "question" that is now clearly noticeable but that we did not attend to at the time of the interviews is that it has two quite different components. The first two sentences, which serve both as transition to and frame for the present interview, are not in question form; they state the topics but they do not ask about them. The question itself is placed in parentheses, a commonly used marker in schedules for designating probes, that is, questions that an interviewer may or may not ask depending on a respondent's response to a core question. In designing this opening comment-cum-

Transcript 1

A Comparison of the Question as Text in the Interview Schedule and Questions Asked by Interviewers

Question as Text

Last time, when we were all together, we covered a lot of ground, from experiences before your marriage up to the present. I would like to begin today with any further thoughts you might have had about any particular events, or experiences, or feelings about what has happened over time in your family and marriage. (What has occurred to you since we last talked about what might have been significant, or what changes have occurred in your lives that was particularly important?)

ML901:H

001	E	This is going to be uh a little bit more (P) formal than
002		last time because I've got a (P) series of questions to go
		[
003	H	Hm hm
004	E	through with you 'n ah but I'd like to begin ah just with
005		a rather general one when we were together last time we
006		covered a lot of ground about all sorts of things
007		about your marriage and your- and your family.
		[
008	H	We sort of rambled around. I got the feeling you
009		weren't getting the answers you wanted. We ran away too much.
		[
010	E	Well there aren't-
011		No there aren't any answers that I *want*.
012	H	Well alright. Fine.
013	E	But ah But I was wondering if we might begin today with
014		any further thoughts you might have had about things we
		[
015	H	Well may-
016	E	talked about (P) last time. Is anything in terms of
		[
017	H	Alright.

```
018  E   your thinking about things we talked about. Is there
019      anything that you've thought about as having been partic-
020      ularly a:ah significant or important about uh your-
021      your family marriage history that-
022  H   (P) We've had ups and downs like everybody else. (P)
023      We had uh four headstrong boys and two girls who were
024      very pliable (P) 'n no problem. They went all the way
025      through college. (Got 'an) education. I couldn't seem
026      to (P) elevate the boys any higher than high school and
027      that's somewhat of a disappointment. They've all got
028      good heads on their shoulders 'n they just bent in other
029      directions. They're all working, they're all hard-
030      self em- (P) they're all gainfully employed, in their
                      [
031  E               Hm hm
032  H   own homes and I-I shouldn't complain.
         (Respondent continues)
```

ML902:H

```
001  E   No that's fine. Just to make sure we're working. Uh
                                                          [
002  H                                                   (. . .)
003  E   Just in the reflecting on- on your past did (P) you
004      think any further about uh parts of it that were partic-
                                                          [
005  H                                                   As to what ah-
006  E   ularly important, or that were significant for you that
                                        [
007  H                                 A:ah
008  E   you hadn't thought about for awhile? Or-
009  H   Actually I- I- I don't think so ah about all- I mean to
010      say what it did do was to bring back memories of- (P) to
011      repeat myself of the past of- y'know how and what we did
012      and- to- sort of one thing it did do I think is (P)
013      remind me that we weren't such *bad* parents and we weren't
014      such bad children (P) to our parents and that ah we uh
015      weren't the worst people in the world y'know you forget a
016      little bit as you get older as to what you yourself have
017      done and ah (P) reflections that I had was that ah our
018      childhood ah growing up we had- ah despite the fact that
```

(Respondent continues)

019		we were poor we weren't lacking any love or anything and
020		uh (P) I mean other than that- I mean I just can't (. . .)
021		y'know- unless (. . .) giving you you know the- the exact

[

| 022 | E | No, that's uh- |
| 023 | H | uh you know things that uh came- come to my mind. |

(*Respondent continues*)

ML901:W

001 A   I think here we go right? Yep. Okay. Now *last time*

[

002 W   (. . .)

003 A   we (h) talked about uh early experiences and I'd like
004   to begin today with any thoughts you may have had about
005   what we *talked* about or- or any events or things that
006   happened in your family and marriage. What *occurred*
007   to you since last- last time we talked about what might
008   have been significant or what changes have occurred in
009   your lives that were particularly important?

[

010 W   I did think it
011   over I think you usually do ah (P) I think for me it
012   identified (P) probably the most difficult time as a
013   family were the middle sixties because of the kids
014   and I think it kind of put it all together for us (P)
015   between you know the kids were on campuses then the
016   time of the draft. (P) I think as a family I think
017   probably (P) the most difficult time that- I- I was
018   terribly conflicted I think during that time.

(*Respondent continues*)

ML902:W

001 A   Here we go. Okay. (P) Now *last* time when we were all
002   together we- uh we talked about a lot of different
003   things. And maybe today we can begin with any further

[

004 W   Uhm:m

005 A   thoughts you might have had about any particular events
006   or experiences or feelings about what happened over the-
007   over time in your family and marriage. (P) Have some-
008   Have some (P) things happened that we missed that you

```
009            decided later was important-
                            [
010    W                          You mean that- that hurt or or happy?
011    A    Well what happened.
012    W    The hurt was since- The hurt was since my father died.
013         I mean an' my whole family just (P) disintegrated. I
014         think that's really the word. That's the biggest hurt
015         that I've ever had in my whole life as far as family.
016         I mean we were very close closely- close family. I
017         just- all it's six years already an'- an' the sad part
018         (P) huh:h when I think about it I get ang- so angry
019         that I- y'know it- when Leslie got married (P) and
020         of course it was my twin brother I should refer to him
021         as Morris he y'know said ('n) invite Mickey an' invite
                    [
022    A               (Laughter)
023    W    this one- I said I can't I can't I just- and I think
024         there was a certain revenge I got that- that I was having
                                        [
025    A                                  And you didn't-
026    W    an affai- a simcha and I didn't invite them.
            (Respondent continues)
```

question, we did not appreciate the possibility that this double structure might make both question and answer problematic. It seems to me now that not only is the range of topics presented wide, but the form of the introduction adds further complexity.

The two interviewers vary in their opening statements and thereby specify the meaning of the text question in different ways. There is variation both between interviewers and within the same interviewer: each asks his and her pair of respondents different questions. In his interview with the first husband, ML901:H, E begins with a transitional and framing comment that is not in the text question. Presumably he is attempting to alert the respondent to the fact that this will be a different type of interview from the previous one by remarking that it will be a "bit more (P) formal" and that he has "a (P) series of questions to {H: Hm hm} go through" (lines 001–004).

The respondent interrupts E's introductory statement with a

comment about the earlier joint interview that is negative in its evaluative tone about both the interviewer's and his own and his wife's behavior—"We sort of rambled around" and "ran away too much"—but he also asserts that E had conveyed the sense that he "wasn't getting the answers [he] wanted" (008–009). E reassures him with a pat interviewer's response to such comments, "No there aren't any answers that I *want*" (011). After receiving acknowledgment of this from the respondent, he then gets to the first question. He transforms the text question, a request for new topics, into a question that focuses narrowly on what had been talked about in the first interview: ". . . begin today with any further thoughts you might have had {H: Well may-} about things we talked about (P) {H: Alright} last time" (013–016). Without waiting for a response, E then opens the question to anything the respondent has "thought about" as significant in the "family marriage history" (019–021).

In contrast, E neither mentions nor directs attention to what was covered the previous week in opening the interview with the second husband, ML902:H. Instead he makes a general request for any further reflections on any "significant" "parts" of his past that he "hadn't thought about for awhile" (003–008). An omission that is particularly striking is that in neither opening question does E include the list of items carefully specified in the text question, namely, events, experiences, or feelings.

In the interview with the first wife, ML901:W, the opening question is both inclusive and open ended. A asks for "any thoughts" about what had been talked about in the first interview "or any events or things that happened in your family or marriage" (003–006). This first statement paraphrases and compresses the beginning of the text question, substituting the vague word *things* for *experiences* and *feelings*, and is consistent with the nonquestion form of the text. She follows this up, without pause and with no acknowledgment from the respondent, with a question that is almost identical with the probe component of the next question (006–009). The identity of phrasing suggests that she is reading from the schedule.

With the second wife, ML902:W, A makes an introductory statement that is more vague in reference to the last interview than is the text question—"we talked about a lot of different things"—but her opening question is almost identical to the first part of the text question—"And maybe today we can begin with any further thoughts you might have had about any particular events or experiences or feelings about what happened over the- over time in your family and marriage" (003–007). After a brief pause where she waits for but receives no immediate response from the respondent, she asks a probe question that changes the topic to "things" not previously talked about: "Have some (P) things happened that we missed that you decided later was important- {W: You mean that- that hurt or or happy?}" (008–010). This approach contrasts with her more direct reliance on the probe question in the other interview.

In these four interviews the questions actually asked differ from the text question and among themselves. The two interviewers ask for "further thoughts" about one or another or sometimes a combination of the following: things talked about in the first interview, important things missed in the first interview, significant parts of the past not thought about for a while, particular events or experiences or feelings occurring at any time in the family and marriage history.

It is evident that the intended meaning of the question as formulated and stated in the interview schedule was specified in different ways for each of the respondents. Earlier I cited Lazarsfeld's (1935, p. 4) advocacy of "a rather loose and liberal handling of a questionnaire by an interviewer" and his general view that it is "much more important that the question be fixed in its *meaning,* than in the *wording.*" Certainly it could be said that the two interviewers in this illustration followed his recommendation. Unfortunately the central issue of whether their different questions had the same meaning to the interviewees is not easily determined. This issue cannot be settled or resolved by flat assertions and ad hoc assumptions but requires systematic analysis, an explicit theory of relations between speech and meaning, and an understanding of interviews as jointly produced discourse.

At a minimum (and this chapter has the restricted aim of making this point in preparation for later analyses) it should be evident that any attempt to ascertain the meaning of questions and responses requires a more adequate description of interviews than is usually provided. At the time Lazarsfeld was writing it was not feasible to tape-record interviews in the field. Tape recorders are now commonplace, but investigators have not yet made tape-recording a necessary and routine feature of standard interview studies. The excerpts used here illustrate ways in which the text version of a question may be transformed in the interview situation. From these examples it is clear that an adequate understanding of what each respondent's answer means—of one having had "ups and downs like everybody else," of another being reminded that "we weren't such *bad* parents and we weren't such bad children," of one feeling the interview had identified "the most difficult time as a family," of another recalling "the biggest hurt that I've ever had in my whole life as far as family"—must begin with the question actually asked as the context for interpreting the response. To assume that the question printed in the schedule is the standard stimulus for all respondents is neither a secure nor a credible basis for analysis and interpretation.

Studies of interviewer reliability in standard surveys, referred to in Chapter 1, indicate that 25–40 percent of the questions asked by interviewers depart significantly from the wording of the questions in the schedule. In the examples used here the two interviewers were the principal investigators, had collaborated on the design and development of the interview schedule, knew and understood the overall aims of the study as well as the aim of this specific question, and had considerable prior experience as researchers and interviewers. We might have expected this combination of involvement, understanding, and experience to have produced closer concordance to the text question and to each other. For this reason we may consider this example an even stronger test of the assumption that the text question can be treated as the question asked. The counterevidence presented here is consistent with the findings from standard surveys and supports the contention that the meaning of questions is problematic and must be ascertained in each instance, that is, in each interview.

Although the text question used in this example is complex and offers the opportunity for interviewers to vary widely in what they emphasize, the argument is intended to be more generally applicable. Ambiguity and complexity are omnipresent in all situations and types of discourse. Shared understanding between speakers and, in interview research, between them and the analyst of survey data depends on a variety of implicit assumptions and on mutual recognition of contextual factors. Gumperz (1982, pp. 166–167) points out that the "labels" participants use for speech activities, in this instance an interview, are not sufficient determinants of how speakers enter the discourse and understand what is being said. Rather, the labels serve only as "guidelines for the interpretation of events which show certain general similarities when considered in the abstract but vary in detail from instance to instance . . . Speech activities are realized in action." Even questions that are apparently simple in both structure and topic leave much room for alternative interpretations by both interviewer and respondent.

Further, open-ended questions in highly regarded surveys of attitudes, motives, and values reveal relatively high levels of complexity in intention and wording. For example, in an early and influential text on survey research Hyman (1955) includes an appendix with copies of interview schedules from the major surveys he uses in his presentation of methods. We find questions such as the following from a national survey of American attitudes toward the atomic bomb.

> Q1. Now that the war is over, how do you feel about the way the countries of the world are getting along together these days?
>
> Q23. Do you think it would be possible to organize the nations of the world in the same way the states in this country are organized, with a government over them all to make laws that they would all have to obey? Why?
>
> Q26. Do you think the discovery of the atomic bomb has made it easier or harder to keep peace in the world? Why?

And from the U.S. Strategic Bombing Survey of Germany:

> Q1. How is it going with you now under the occupation?
>
> Q45. What in your opinion was the chief cause of the war?

Q57. Could you explain to me in a few words how you reacted to the evacuation?

Survey questions do not appear to get less complex over the years. Veroff, Douvan, and Kulka (1981) include their interview schedule as appendix A in their report of changes in American attitudes over a twenty-year period. Typical in the degree of complexity of form and meaning of their open-ended questions are the following.

C1. Everybody has some things he worries about more or less. What kinds of things do you worry about most?
C6. Everyone has things about their life they're not completely happy about. What are some of the things you're not too happy about these days? (Probe for full responses.)
F1. First thinking about a man's/woman's life. How is a man's/woman's life changed by being married? (Probe for feelings.)
F7. Every marriage has its good points and bad points. What things about your marriage are not quite as nice as you would like them to be? (Probe for full responses.)

These types of questions are not atypical in surveys of attitudes on significant personal, political, and social issues. If one considers how an interviewer might paraphrase, rephrase, or elaborate such questions when a respondent asks for clarification or does not respond in a clearly adequate way, one can see how these questions leave considerable room for interviewer variation. The ubiquity in these questions of the indexical term *things* is particularly noticeable in this regard. This term takes on specific meaning only when a context has been provided. Interviewers and respondents in the give-and-take of the interview must provide the context giving the term a meaning that is shared sufficiently for them to continue talking together. Unfortunately, their exchanges are not available to coders and data analysts, who must then introduce contexts in order to "make sense" of the responses.

Although I have been focusing on the complexity and ambiguity of the questions themselves, it is particularly important to recognize that question form is not the determining factor in the process through which ambiguity is manifested and resolved. This is done through the way that interviewers and respondents attempt to "fit" their questions and responses to each other and to the developing discourse. Presumably "simple" questions are as open and sensitive to this process as are complex ones. Ambiguities are resolved through the discourse itself and not by efforts to give a more precise statement to questions in the interview schedule.

These problems generally are not topics for reflection and analysis within the mainstream tradition. Instead they are removed from the observational field through assumptions about standard interviewer performance embodied, for example, in Hyman's (1955, pp. 367–368) description of the method of interviewing used in the study of attitudes toward the atomic bomb: "The interviewers were instructed to ask the questions exactly as they were stated, but to use additional 'non-directive' probes, such as 'Why is that?', 'Why do you feel that way?', etc. wherever necessary in order to obtain as clear a picture as possible of the individual's reasoning. Each answer was recorded as nearly verbatim as possible." The interviews presented in Transcript 1 strongly suggest that this instruction be read as an expression of hopefulness rather than as a description of actual interviewer performance.

Taking speech seriously requires investigators to pay close attention to linguistic and paralinguistic features that appear routinely in naturally occurring talk but are routinely omitted from standard written texts. The transcripts presented here, for example, include certain details of speech, such as pauses, nonlexical expressions, and speaker interruptions and overlaps, that are rarely found even in illustrative excerpts in reports of interview studies. Transcribing tape-recorded interviews is complex, tedious, and time-consuming work that demands careful listening and relistening, the use of explicit transcription rules, and a well-specified notation system. Attempting to prepare a reasonably adequate transcription of an interview will convince any investigator of the significance of these routinely omitted features for understanding the meaning of what is said.

The complexity of the task of transcribing speech into written text merits brief comment. There are many ways to prepare a transcript and each is only a partial representation of speech. Further, and most important, each representation is also a transformation. That is, each transcript includes some and excludes other features of speech and rearranges the flow of speech into lines of text within the limits of a page. Some features of speech, such as rapid changes in pitch, stress, volume, and rate, seem almost impossible to represent adequately while at the same time retaining the legibility of the text. Adding another complexity are the nonlinguistic features of any speech situation, such as gestures, facial expressions, body movements, that are not captured on audiotape recordings and are difficult to describe and record from observations or videotapes. Lastly, it must be borne in mind that the initial record—audio- or videotape or running observation—is itself only a partial representation of what "actually" occurred.

These cautionary remarks are not intended to discourage investigators but to alert them to problems that must be explicitly faced and resolved in each particular study. As I have noted before, viewing interviews as discourse brings into the foreground problems that have been shunted aside by the mainstream approach; problems of transcription do not arise if interviews are not recorded and if questions and answers are viewed as stimulus-response pairs.

That transcription problems are inherently insoluble in any sense of completeness suggests certain guidelines for preparing and using transcripts. First, investigators must keep in mind that speech is the intended object of study. At each stage of analysis and interpretation they must be wary of taking their own transcripts too seriously as *the* reality. Transcripts tend to take on a life of their own, especially given the effort, attention, and time involved in their preparation and analysis. Their form—how lines are arranged and how overlaps in speech and interruptions are marked, whether pauses are simply noted or measured in tenths of seconds—both expresses prior assumptions about the nature of talk and generates new hypotheses. For these reasons it is important to keep returning to the original recordings to assess the adequacy of an interpretation.

Second, because there is no universal form of transcription that is adequate for all research questions and settings, the criteria for choice are theoretical concerns and practical constraints. The mode of transcription adopted should reflect and be sensitive to an investigator's general theoretical model of relations between meaning and speech, selectively focus on aspects of speech that bear directly on the specific aims of the study, and take into consideration the limitations of the basic data and of resources available for analysis.[3]

The experience of transcribing is also likely to convince investigators of the need for repeated listenings to ensure the most accurate transcript possible for their own analytic purposes, irrespective of the notation system chosen. For example, the excerpts in Transcript 1 passed through several stages before reaching their current state—a first draft prepared by an experienced typist shortly after the interviews were conducted; a revision shortly thereafter, based on my relistening to the tapes; a second revision six years later, prepared by me and involving several relistenings of the sections presented here; and a third revision based on multiple relistenings by members of my research seminar.

Did these revisions lead to any significant changes in meaning, that is, in what we as investigators understood of what was said? Unequivocally the answer is yes. In line 001 of the interview with ML901:H, the word "formal" after a pause appeared in the first typescript as "informal," was changed at my first relistening to "formal," was changed back to "informal" in my second revision years later, and was changed to "formal" again after my seminar's hearing of the tape. The respondent's comment "We sort of rambled around" in line 008 of the same interview was omitted and marked as unclear talk, "(. . .)", in the draft and first revision; my later hearing of it as this statement was confirmed in the seminar's listening. In lines 030–032 the phrase "in their own homes" was heard by me in the second revision as "own their own homes" but was then changed back to its current version in the seminar. And in line 018 of the interview with ML901:W the word "conflicted" appeared as "concerned" in the first draft. It is, I think, evident that there is a difference in meaning between "informal" and "formal" and between "conflicted" and "concerned."

A particularly dramatic example of the importance of relistening was brought to my attention recently by Linda Isaacs (personal communication). She conducted a series of intensive unstructured interviews with women who had undergone prenatal diagnostic procedures. Her typists were given little instruction beyond the general one to include "everything" that was said the way it was said. The draft typescript of one interview includes the respondent's assertion that she knew the exact moment that she "got pregnant." The transcript then moves on to another topic. On relistening to the tape, Dr. Isaacs discovered that the typist had omitted in its entirety an extended statement by the respondent, following her assertion, of the reasons for her certainty, including her visual imagery of her conception and pregnancy and her confounding of physicians who had reported negative results of the first pregnancy test. From relistening to the tapes and editing the transcripts, Dr. Isaacs observed that the material "filtered out" by her typists often turned out to be of special significance for understanding respondents' experiences.

Despite all the difficulties noted here, I wish to reemphasize the point that systematic transcription procedures are necessary for valid analysis and interpretation of interview data. This recommendation is neither an easy nor an economical one to follow. Some minimum level of detail is required for any study, but how fine this detail must be depends on the aims of the particular study and remains a matter of judgment. It seems clear, however, that the value of succeeding stages of a study—coding, analysis, and interpretation—depends on the adequacy of the description of the phenomenon of interest, and in interview research this means a carefully prepared transcript.

I began by redefining interviews as speech events. Examining them as such has led us back to the interviews themselves, to actual questions and responses of interviewers and respondents. This direction of movement is in direct contrast to the standard approach, which relies on the question as printed in the schedule and on interviewers' written on-the-spot accounts. The inadequacies of the latter approach were documented by examples of departures from text questions both by the same interviewer and by different interviewers. Such departures are not exceptions but rather are representative of a process that is inherent to interviewing, regardless of the particular form and intent of a question. They are a necessary feature of the process of discourse.

This chapter's limited aim was to show that the meanings of questions and answers are problematic. Questions in the interview schedule and interviewers' summaries do not adequately represent what is actually said, and it is only through knowing what they say that we can begin to address the question of what they mean. This question is central to the approach to interviewing presented in the following chapters.

3

The Joint Construction
of Meaning

In this chapter I explore implications of the proposition stated earlier that the discourse of the interview is jointly constructed by interviewer and respondent. I will show how both questions and responses are formulated in, developed through, and shaped by the discourse between interviewers and respondents. Further, I will argue that an adequate understanding of interviews depends on recognizing how interviewers reformulate questions and how respondents frame answers in terms of their reciprocal understanding as meanings emerge during the course of an interview.

Variations among interviewers and across interviews such as those discussed in Chapter 2 are not viewed here as "errors" but as significant "data" for analysis. In the standard approach differences in how interviewers ask questions are treated as technical problems that can be "solved" by obeying various rules and prescriptions for question wording and interviewer performance. (See Brenner, 1985, p. 19, for a particularly detailed list of "rules" for reducing the "biasing effects of inadequate interviewer performance.") In my view such variation is endemic and unavoidable, and the documented failure of technical solutions reveals that the requirement of standardization cannot be fulfilled in practice. Further, the narrowly technical approach removes the problem of how questions are asked from the interview context. It excludes from consideration the course of the interview itself, that it, the internal history of the developing discourse, which is shaped by prior exchanges between interviewer and respondent. Within the perspective of interviews as speech events and speech activities, variation in how particular questions are asked as well as variation in the overall course of interviews become objects of inquiry. Because we cannot ascertain the meaning of a question simply by referring to the interview schedule and interviewer's notes, the research question is transformed from a search for "errors" to an analysis of the interview process in order to determine the meaning of questions and answers.

One way an interview develops is through mutual reformulation and specification of questions, by which they take on particular and context-bound shades of meaning. This process is illustrated by an exchange in the interview with ML902:W given in Transcript 1 of Chapter 2. In line 010 the respondent specifies the meaning of the interviewer's general question about important events in her family and marriage by proposing her own question, "You mean that- that hurt or happy?" The interviewer appears to accept this specific formulation of the question by asking the respondent to continue, "Well what happened." The respondent replies, "The hurt was since- The hurt was since my father died." Understanding the meaning of this respondent's "answer" depends on our recognizing it as an answer to her own specification of the question rather than to the original question asked by the interviewer. I am not suggesting that "The hurt was since my father died" is not a response, and an adequate and appropriate one, to the original question. But that question has many possible meanings through which its intention may be realized, and in this exchange it has taken on only one meaning, the one specified by the respondent and accepted in turn by the interviewer. Rather than serving as a stimulus having a predetermined and presumably shared meaning and intended to elicit a response, a question may more usefully be thought of as part of a circular process through which its meaning and that of its answer are created in the discourse between interviewer and respondent as they try to make continuing sense of what they are saying to each other.

In this example the respondent's role in redefining the question is quite evident. Often, of course, the interviewer's definition appears to be dominant. Even in these instances, however, it is important to recognize that acquiescence by respondents represents active participation on their part in the construction of the meaning of questions. That is, respondents learn from how interviewers respond to their answers—restating or rephrasing the original question, accepting the answer and going on to the next question, probing for further information—what particular meanings are intended by questions and wanted in their answers in a particular interview context. Respondents' acceptance of interviewers' frameworks of meanings is a key factor in a "successful" interview. Agreement by respondents to cooperate with interviewers and do what they are asked to do is often seen as the essential but *only* requirement for adequate participation. Thus Brenner (1985, p. 19), while viewing the set of rules he offers for interviewers as "comprehensive," remarks that "there are no particular rules for the respondent (besides the 'weak' rule that he should provide adequate answers, having agreed to the interview)." Recalcitrant respondents, those who refuse to learn and follow the rules of this game, may produce "answers" that are uncodable and therefore likely to be discarded in later analyses.

The pattern of interviewer dominance and respondent acquiescence is well documented in medical interviews, where asymmetry in power is especially clear. Although medical interviews differ from standard research interviews in several important respects, the two are similar in that both are methodic inquiries in which interviewers through a series of questions attempt to elicit "relevant" information from respondents. The excerpt in Transcript 2 is adapted from Mishler (1984, typescript 3.2). It demonstrates how an interviewer/physician "teaches" a respondent/patient to restrict answers to only that information the physician considers relevant, namely, to shift from initial extended responses to simple yes or no answers.

The transcript begins with the doctor's (D) first question

(00l–002), which followed immediately after he initiated the interview by asking for the patient's (P) name. The question includes a series of unrelated diseases, "tuberculosis diabetes (acantees) suicide," and refers to relatives rather than the patient himself. Although the question would be satisfied by a simple yes or no answer, the patient appears to treat it as an open-ended request for his family medical history and refers to one of the specified diseases. Attempting to be accurate, he reports the specific time and circumstances of his father's tuberculosis. The physician checks the time of occurrence (007), attempts to interrupt the extended account (010), and then indicates that the patient's response is irrelevant, restricting the original question to "the last ten years" and a relationship of intimate association (011–012). The patient limits his next response to a simple no (013). This first restricted answer is preceded by a brief pause, as if he is still uncertain about how to respond. The physician's succeeding questions each include multiple illnesses or organs and are asked at a rapid pace with no intervening pause after the previous answer. Having learned that all that is required of him is a straightforward positive or negative response, the patient answers equally rapidly; none of these later answers is preceded by a pause.

It seemed evident in the original analysis of this interview that the physician was filling in an insurance form or other type of standard medical questionnaire. The patient recognizes, from the content and pacing of the physician's questions and probably as well from observing him checking off the answers, that little detail is required. In this respect the patient is acting in the same way that respondents act in research interviews. Although the physician's framework of intentions and meanings is dominant, the patient and physician are together jointly constructing a discourse that takes a particular form.

The lesson of this example is that responses are not simply answers to questions but also a reflection of the interviewer's assessment of whether a respondent has said "enough" for the purpose at hand. These assessments may be quite explicit, as in this physician's limiting of the question to a specific time period, or more implicit, as in the close timing and rapid pacing of his

Transcript 2

The Medical Interview: A Physician's Question and the
Restriction of a Patient's Responses

W:02.013

```
001  D   Have there any cases of tuberculosis diabetes (acantees)
002      suicide among your relatives.
003  P                            (h) ...... (h) My father
004      had tuberculosis oh:h .......... tst . twenty ohgee twenty
005      five thirty years ago he was in the hospital ..........
006      he was there two years.
007  D                           Twenty five years ago herng:h?
008  P   ........ Oh maybe longer than that. (h) I was a little boy.
009      Twenty five- Yeah I'd say twenty five years ago.
                    [
010  D           (...)                                 ........
011      Have you (within) the last ten years been intimately as-
012      sociated with anyone having tuberculosis?
013  P                                      .... No.
014  D                                          Have
015      you ever consulted a doctor suffered from any illnesses
016      or diseases of the brain or the nervous system?
017  P                                          No.
018  D                                          Heart
019      blood vessels or lungs?
020  P                    N:no.
021  D                         Stomach or intestines.
022  P                                      No.
023  D   Skin glands (nurr) your *eyes*?
024  P                    No.
025  D                             Have you ever had rheuma-
026      tism bone disease or syphilis.
027  P                    No.
028  D                             Have you ever seen a
029      doctor suffered from any illness or disease not included
030      in the above questions other than for routine colds.
031  P                                          No.
```

successive questions. Tim Anderson (personal communication) has pointed out to me how an even more implicit response by an interviewer, namely, silence, may influence a respondent's answer. When interviewing individuals with chronic pain he asks open-ended questions about their experiences and how they cope with their problems. If he remains silent after the initial response, neither explicitly acknowledging or commenting on the answer nor proceeding immediately to a next question, respondents tend to hesitate, show signs of searching for something else to say, and usually continue with additional content. Sometimes they look for a sign that the interviewer understands or try to elicit a direct assessment with a query like "You know?" Their "answers" are as responsive to his assessments as to the original questions. They display the respondents' effort to arrive at a shared understanding of the meaning of both questions and answers.

Another example of how responses, even in interviews that are intentionally unstructured and open ended, may be influenced by a priori assumptions about adequacy as well as the practical exigencies of a study was brought to my attention by Susan Bell (personal communication). In her interviews with daughters of women who had taken the drug DES (diethylstilbestrol) during pregnancy to prevent miscarriage, Bell (1983) asks a question drawn from Gilligan's (1982) work, "How would you describe yourself to yourself?" Her respondents give extended accounts, often generating several pages of transcript. Such a large amount of data poses serious difficulties for analysis. Bell asked other investigators who had used the same question in their studies of women's development how they approached this problem and discovered that they rely on experienced interviewers to learn how to get briefer responses to this question so as to avoid the problem. In other words, despite their interest in having women tell their own stories in their own ways, some investigators carried into the interview a set of assumptions and implicit criteria about the adequacy of a response. Respondents, for their part, learned during the interview how to answer adequately, but briefly.

Gilligan (1982) provides an instructive example of what may

happen in an interview when differences are not resolved between an interviewer and respondent in their respective understandings of a question's meaning. She argues that the questions
in the standard moral-development interview and the coding
manual for responses (Kohlberg, 1969; Kohlberg and Kramer,
1969) incorporate a particular ideology and theory about both
morality and development that is consistent with how boys tend
to view the world but inconsistent with how girls think. One
widely used question refers to the moral dilemma faced by Heinz,
whose wife is dying of a serious illness. He cannot afford to buy
the drug that might help her, and the druggist refuses his request
for it. The issue posed to respondents is whether Heinz should
steal the drug. Gilligan describes an eleven-year-old girl's problem with this question and with the interview as a whole: "Failing
to see the dilemma as a self-contained problem in moral logic, she
does not discern the internal structure of its resolution; as she
constructs the problem differently herself, Kohlberg's conception completely evades her" (Gilligan, 1982, p. 29).

The interviewer is frustrated by the girl's apparent inability to
understand and answer his questions. Gilligan reverses the
source of the problem and points instead to "the interviewer's
inability to understand her response" and to the way he "conveys through the repetition of questions that the answers she
gave were not heard or not right" (p. 29). Although this girl
does not yield to the interviewer's conception of the question
and the moral dilemma it poses, her confidence in her own
replies diminishes. As the interview continues her responses
become constrained, repetitious, and unsure. In the end her
responses, generated by an interviewer who is not responsive to
her understanding, result in a lower rating on the moral-
development scale applied to such interviews than those received by children who accept the question in the interviewer's
terms. Again, this specific result does not differ from the standard procedure in interview research of coding respondents'
answers as if they had been produced by an isolated speaker
responding to a stimulus-question rather than through the complex discourse of the interview.

These examples suggest a variety of ways through which the

meanings of questions and responses may be achieved, from successive reformulations by interviewers and respondents until they arrive at an acceptable level of shared agreement to the insistence of interviewers on their definitions. However understandings are arrived at, residues of disagreement and uncertainty may remain. The process of negotiating meaning is brushed aside in the standard approach, in which responses tend to be coded and analyzed as if they were "answers" to preformulated questions.

On some occasions even the apparent achievement of agreement remains in doubt. For example, in the interviews with husbands and wives discussed in Chapter 2 interviewers asked respondents to locate the high and low points in their marriage. The question was intended primarily as a screening question, that is, to provide interviewers with contrasts in satisfaction about which a series of open-ended questions could be asked, such as, "What was going on during that time that made it a high/low point?" "Were there any other important changes in your life situation or in your activities during that time?" This question is not unusual in interviews about marriage and family life. The survey interview used by Veroff, Douvan, and Kulka (1981) includes: "F6. We've talked a little about marriage in general. Now, thinking about your own marriage, what would you say are the nicest things about it? (Probe: Anything else?). F7. Every marriage has its good points and bad points. What things about your marriage are not quite as nice as you would like them to be? (Probe for full responses)."

Initially we assumed that the terms *high* and *low points* were relatively straightforward and at the same time sufficiently open for respondents to define them in their own ways. As it turned out, respondents found this a difficult question. Transcript 3 records the efforts of one interviewer and respondent to clarify the meaning of the question and to reach a level of shared understanding that would permit relevant and adequate responses. As will be evident, it remains uncertain whether this level was reached. (In this transcript, and in later ones, the length of pauses is marked by dots, each one representing one-tenth of a second.)

Transcript 3

The Joint Construction by Interviewers and Respondents
of the Meaning of Questions

Question as Text

Now would you look at this chart which lists the dates of your
marriage and other events you have just told me. Near the top is
a line for the first year of your marriage; each line is for another
year of your marriage up to the present. Would you first put an
"X" on the lines for those years that you feel were the high points
of your marriage and family life, the years that you now feel were
the happiest and the most satisfying for you. Use the right-hand
column for this. (If R states that all years/or many years were high
points, ask: Could you pick out the 3 or 4 years, or periods of
time, that were the highest points?) (If R states that there were no
high points, ask: Could you pick out the 3 or 4 years or periods of
time that were the best, or better than other times?) When R
finishes checking high points: Would you do the same thing for
what you feel were the years or times that were the low points, the
years that you feel were the least satisfying or most troubling
times in your marriage and family life. (Same probe questions as
for high points.)

ML901:H

001	E	Uh, what I'd like to do now is to go through this, this
002		is just this time chart which is sort of filled in with
003		a few of these dates to give a sense of the first year
004		of your marriage down through the 1976, right now. And
005		what I'd like are times that were high points or low points
006		in the marriage history and if you would just check on that
007		column the high points on the right. What some of the years
008		or lots of years were that you remember as being particu-
009		larly satisfying, a high point is a rough way of putting
010		it, but as you reflect back on it what would be the best
011		time for your marriage.
012	H	.. Well the best times were the years
013		that the children were growing up (.. R continues ..) how do

```
014         you want me- just put a check?
015    E                              Well just put a check mark
016         down either on the years or the stretches of years that
017         you thought were- I'm gonna ask you to pick out some of
018         the low points also so-
019    H                         I'm checking the wrong places.
020         .......... In terms of- If you want a literal interpreta-
021         tion of a high point I can't seem to make too much dif-
022         ferentiation between the two. We went through a period
023         where you know we didn't have any money (.. R continues ..)
024    E    You wouldn't call those times troubling times? Low
025         points in that sense?
026    H                         Well they- they were troubling times
027         no, they weren't troubles in the sense of real troubles
028         no, but they were en- en- enforced lean times (.. R
029         continues with extended account of the cost of medical
030         care for a sick child ..)
031    E    (...) Part of the question is what would you count as
032         high points or low points of your and what's the meaning
033         (...)
034    H      Well that would be a low point. Is ah these are
035         high points, there are definitely high points .. the
036         first .. and these were kind of-
                                            [
037    E                              Not every year has to be
038         a high or a low point.
039    H                         No I know. I- I can't make a
040         tangible construction out of this in terms of definitive
041         high points and low points. It just doesn't make that-
042         my feeling about it is in thinking about it is amorphous,
043         I just cannot come down on anything solid. ah
044    E                                             .. Well
045         let me ask you the question a little bit differently,
046         since this is really to get on to some other kinds of
047         questions. If you think back maybe five or six years
048         ago ah to the time that you think of as being a partic-
049         ularly good time, either a good year or some stretch
050         of time, that you might think of as being what I'm calling
051         a high point.
052    H                         .. Oh well there was- there was a time I-
```

(Respondent continues)

053		I started my own business ah, and ah, and like anything
054		as you might expect there were- there were very trying
055		times and that was ah- ... was ah say ah (...) years ago.
056		Probably 1966.
057	E	That would be what you call a low point?

Although the respondent begins quite firmly, "Well the best times were the years that the children were growing up" (012–013), he almost immediately encounters difficulty, "If you want a literal interpretation of a high point I can't seem to make too much differentiation between the two" (020–022). In response to the interviewer's next specific question about whether difficult financial periods should be counted as "troubling times" or "low points in that sense?" (024–025), he says, "Well they-they were troubling times no, they weren't troubles in the sense of real troubles no, but they were en- en- enforced lean times" (026–028). He then proceeds with a lengthy and irrelevant story (irrelevant to the interviewer's purpose for asking the question) about how during a financially bad time he paid off a large physician's bill through small monthly installments. The apparent intent of the story is to demonstrate to the interviewer how he turned a low point into a high point, that is, how he succeeded against adversity.[1]

The terms of the question continue to remain unclear or unacceptable to the respondent, who says he "can't make a tangible construction out of this in terms of definitive high points and low points" (039–041). The interviewer tries several times to restate the question. In his last response in this excerpt the respondent begins to talk about a recent high point (047–051) but then quickly indicates that it was "very trying times" (054–055). Small wonder that the interviewer's final question is marked by confusion, "That would be what you call a low point?" (057).

Similar difficulties with this question appear in the other interviews in this series. For example, the respondent ML901:W begins carefully to consider each year on the time chart, which shows the dates of important events such as the birthdates of children. She asks, "Fallow places don't count do they?" Knowing that this question is intended only as a screening question, the interviewer attempts to make the respondent answer more quickly: "Well what we can do is uhm - [W: I can tell you ah-] If you can pick out three or four periods of the - of the highest points."

Another respondent, ML902:H, quickly lists the first, fifth, twenty-fifth, and thirtieth years of his marriage as high points and then says, "I can't really think of any high points other than that." In response to the interviewer's question "How about low points?" he remembers to add births of his son and daughter as additional high points. Responding to the interviewer's next question, a rephrased effort to elicit low points, he says "Y'know I'm just trying to think, ah when we got married I say the first year of marriage was exciting because we were married but it wasn't because of the fact that her mother was sick when we did get married and of course my mother when she died that certainly wasn't happy, I can't think of real low points ah I would say generally speaking, it may not be high points or low points, nothing really came easy to us. To me especially, I've struggled all my life." After reporting persistent disappointments in his work and his feelings of having missed success, he goes on: "This part has been a low point to me the disappointment of it of all this which would- I could put a low point, but this wouldn't be because of the marriage? [E: Right (. . .)]" The interviewer both reassures and refocuses the question: "No it could be in general although I think- are there times within the family and the marriage that (. . .)-"

Another respondent, ML902:W, indicates how the perception of a period as a high or low point might change with time. In response to a question about any other "high point years you'd want to list" she states: "(. . .) Ah no, ah I think nothing extraordinary. I thought when my daughter started going with her husband y'know and it looked like it might be something y'know and- [A: When was that?] Ah, she'll be married, ah she'll be married three years in October and she went with him for three years so it would be about '71. Of course then I can't say that was a high point because it looked like it might not be anything."

The sustained effort in these several interviews to achieve a shared understanding, within and across interviews, of what is meant by high and low points is remarkably unsuccessful. I doubt that alternative phrasings such as "nicest things" or "good points and bad points" would be less ambiguous. Standard research practice ignores this ambiguity and also the process of disambiguation, sometimes unsuccessful, that takes place in discourse. Terms such as *high point* or *nicest things* are given meanings within the evolving contexts of particular interviews. For one of these respondents, all life has been a struggle punctuated by special positive events such as marriage, anniversaries, and the births of children but, given the complexity of life, even these events are shadowed by the pain of illness and death. For another, whether a specific event or time was a high or low point depends on its later consequences, so how could one know at the time whether it was one or the other? For a third, reporting low points would signify inadequacy or failure so they must quickly be discounted by showing how troubles were overcome. Assessing meaning, as I have repeatedly urged, requires analyzing the interview process so that we can begin to understand how meaning is grounded in and constructed through the discourse.

The examples presented in this chapter demonstrate through their particulars the general proposition that language is inherently indexical.[2] That is, meanings in discourse are neither singular nor fixed, as they are in a fully specified computer program or in a closed set of mathematical axioms and theorems. Rather, terms take on specific and contextually grounded meanings within and through the discourse as it develops and is shaped by speakers. Further, as Connell and Goot (1972–73)[3] point out in their incisive critique of "political socialization" research, serious questions must be raised about the validity of the usual assumption of a "community of meaning" between researchers and respondents and among respondents. Connell and Goot observe that investigators "have assumed that all the children understand the questions in the same way, mean the same thing by their answers, and mean the same thing that the researchers would have meant" (p. 174). They argue that what is meant by questions and answers in interviews must itself be investigated; although their focus is on children's political attitudes and values, their conclusion is widely applicable.

Clearly this chapter makes the same point. I have shown how interviewers and respondents, through repeated reformulations of questions and responses, strive to arrive together at meanings that both can understand. The relevance and appropriateness of questions and responses emerges through and is realized in the discourse itself. The standard approach to the analysis of interviews abstracts both questions and responses from this process. By suppressing the discourse and by assuming shared and standard meanings, this approach short-circuits the problem of meaning. As I suggested earlier, interpretation relies on a variety of implicit assumptions and ad hoc hypotheses. To come to a more adequate understanding of what respondents mean and to develop stronger theories as well as more valid generalizations in interview research, we must attend to the discursive nature of the interview process.

Language, Meaning, and Narrative Analysis

Interview Responses as Stories

The approach to interviewing I have been proposing takes as its fundamental problem the ways that meaning is expressed in and through discourse. It directs attention to the complex sets of linguistic and social rules that structure and guide meaningful talk between speakers. The essential features of interviews as speech events or activities and as jointly constructed discourse were discussed in preceding chapters. With that background we may turn now to the third premise, namely, that analysis and interpretation of interviews are based on a theory of discourse and meaning. By this I mean that interpretation of the organization and patterning of speech depends on a theoretical framework that entails specifying the presuppositions and rules that people use in speaking with one another. I have argued that in the mainstream approach, in which the discursive nature of interviews is obscured or suppressed, implicit assumptions about discourse and meaning enter into analysis and interpretation, and necessarily so. Here the task is to make explicit the theoretical basis of interpretation.

It is important to take note at the outset of the many different forms and functions of language. For example, through language we describe objects and events, explain how something works and why something has happened, express feelings and beliefs, develop logical arguments, persuade others to a course of action, and narrate experiences. Each of these functions has a different structure. In this chapter I focus on one possible form of speech, that is, on interviewee responses as narrative accounts or stories.[1]

Treating responses as stories opens up many complex analytic problems and, of course, it represents only one of a number of approaches to issues of meaning. Choosing it over the others serves several purposes. First, applying story-analysis methods and displaying the findings they generate moves the discussion of interviewing beyond the boundaries set by the traditional approach. To this point my critique of standard research practice and my recommendations for an alternative approach have remained fairly close to the formulation of problems within the mainstream tradition. For example, I examined the problem of meaning in the limited context of interviewees' efforts to understand and respond to specific questions. Looking at how interviewees connect their responses into a sustained account, that is, a story, brings out problems and possibilities of interviewing that are not visible when attention is restricted to question-answer exchanges.

Second, by comparing different approaches and studies, all within the general domain of narrative analysis, I hope to sharpen our understanding of the relations between methods of analysis and underlying "theories" of discourse and meaning. For example, a general assumption of narrative analysis is that telling stories is one of the significant ways individuals construct and express meaning. This assumption informs work by many investigators from a variety of disciplines having different theoretical perspectives.

Rayfield (1972, p. 1085), an anthropologist, refers to "the assumption that there exists universally in the human mind the concept of a certain structure that we call a story" and that in the same way that deep structures of grammar are "built into the human mind," "the story is similarly a natural psychological unit." Gee (1985, p. 11), a linguist, asserts: "One of the primary ways—probably *the* primary way—human beings make sense of their experience is by casting it in a narrative form . . . This is an ability that develops early and rapidly in children, without explicit training or instruction." Cohler (1982), a psychoanalytically oriented psychologist, refers to personal narratives as "the most internally consistent interpretation of presently understood past, experienced present, and anticipated future" (p. 207); he argues for a narrative approach to the study of personality because it "parallels the approach actually used by persons in the successive interpretations or reconstructions of their own history as a personal narrative across the course of life" (p. 229). McAdams (1985, p. 18), proposing the "story metaphor" as a theoretical construct for study of identity development, states that: "identity stability is longitudinal consistency in the life story." Jameson (1981, p. 13), a literary critic, refers to the "all-informing process of *narrative*" as the "central function or *instance* of the human mind." And MacIntyre (1981), a moral philosopher, asserts: "It is because we all live out narratives in our lives and because we understand our own lives in terms of the narratives we live out that the form of narratives is appropriate for understanding the actions of others. Stories are lived before they are told—except in the case of fiction" (p. 197). "What is better or worse for X depends upon the character of that intelligible narrative which provides X's life with its unity" (p. 209). These statements might be multiplied quite easily, but they suffice to show that there is a wide recognition of the special importance of narrative as a mode through which individuals express their understanding of events and experiences.[2]

Third, giving serious attention to stories as topics for investigation makes us reexamine some of the core presuppositions and aims of standard interviewing practice, where respondents' stories are suppressed in that their responses are limited to "relevant" answers to narrowly specified questions. If storytelling and story comprehension are natural and pervasive modes of communicating meaning, and if the suppression of respondents' stories is a central feature of the traditional approach, then giving story analysis a prominent place has broad implications for interview research. These implications are discussed in this chapter and in the following chapter on the contextual grounding of meaning.

Telling stories is far from unusual in everyday conversation and it is apparently no more unusual for interviewees to respond to questions with narratives if they are given some room to speak. This assertion is based on what I have learned from interviews conducted by other investigators[3] as well as my own studies. In general, researchers in the mainstream tradition either have not recognized the pervasiveness of stories because, as I have already remarked, the standard survey interview "suppresses" them, or have treated stories as a problem because they are difficult to code and quantify. We are more likely to find stories reported in studies using relatively unstructured interviews where respondents are invited to speak in their own voices, allowed to control the introduction and flow of topics, and encouraged to extend their responses. Nonetheless respondents may also tell stories in response to direct, specific questions if they are not interrupted by interviewers trying to keep them to the "point."

Before proceeding to a discussion of different approaches to narrative analysis, the reader will find it useful to take a preliminary look at the phenomenon itself, that is, at a respondent's story. In Chapter 3 I used an excerpt (Transcript 3) to show how the meaning of a question is constructed through discourse between interviewer and interviewee. At one point in the transcript I noted a deletion from the respondent's full answer, referring to it in parentheses as an "extended account of the cost of medical care for a sick child" (028–030). In discussing the interview I observed that the section was deleted because I originally felt that it was irrelevant to the specific aim of the question. Indeed, the deleted section is a story and is presented in Transcript 4.

Recall that this extended account, taking slightly over seven minutes, is in response to a request for the respondent to select specific times in his marriage that he would consider high or low points. The question was not open ended; it directed his attention to a time line of his marriage on which significant life changes had been marked. I have already mentioned that the

Transcript 4

A Story Embedded in a Response to a Question

ML901:H

001	E	You wouldn't call those times though troubling times? Uh low
002		points in that sense?
003	H	Well they were- they were troubling times
004		no, they weren't troubles in the sense of real troubles no, but
005		they were en- en- enforced *lean* times (E: Hm hm) where I can
006		remember when the kids were young, I wanted to own a boat in the
007		worst way I didn't care if it cost a hundred dollars I wanted a
008		boat. I was into things during that (...) I think that one of
009		the single things held me back more than anything else, the feeling
010		of financial s- security. It always seemed to be absent. (P)
011		Yet we always *did* what we had to do some*how* we did it. We got
012		through it. ah Danny got severely burned and uh had to have skins-
013		a skin graft and uh surgery and was in the hospital for forty five
014		days and it was expensive and the uh expense of the- of the chil-
015		dren and childbirth and so forth went from I think with Suzy the
016		first one something like six dollars up into a couple of thousand
017		dollars.
018	E	(Heh heh) Six dollars sounds incredible.
019	H	(...) The Blue
020		Cross Blue Shield covered everything for her except six dollars,
021		(E: hh) at Maintown Hospital. They were all born at Maintown.
022		And uh when Richard was admitted (P) ah that would be ah (P) (...)
023		that was a particularly bad time. When Richard was- When Nancy
024		was admitted to the hospital with Richard, they discovered she had
025		a blood clot in her legs, in her vein, did surgery on her at twenty
026		nine so I (guess) that probably saved her life. They did a ligation
027		and (P) and that uh took a year to pay that off. It was one of
028		those things where you religiously had to whack away thirty dollars
029		every week or every two weeks or something. I remember one time
030		when Danny was severely burned, we had a doctor here by the name
031		of- of William Turner affiliated with Northgate Hospital to do the
032		skin graft on the boy and he lives right up the street here. And
033		I- somehow or other, he- he imparted *massive* confidence to me.
034		I would put myself in his care *any* day, *any* day. Whatever that
035		man said it- he seemed to come down right on the right place.

```
036   E                                                          They
037         take special courses in that in medical school, doctor's presence.
                                                                 (
038   H                                                 Do you? uh huh
039         (E: Heh heh) Well he was a- a very rugged 'n short uh extremely
040         uh athletic man uh uh wavy blond hair and he had- He wrestled
041         and did gymnastics and like he- he- built like a flying wedge.
042         And he was- he was rather short. And Danny got a- this terrible
043         burn, his clothing caught fire and he lost all the skin up here,
044         from the top of his ankle all up here. Danny's upstairs somewhere
045         in bed, he's got the flu (...) And they did a graft from here
046         down to here. And I remember being so concerned about it, but
047         anyhow I think Bill Turner- the whole bill came to fifteen hun-
048         dred dollars. Everything. (P) (...) and it came in at a time
049         when we were just taking on a second mortgage on the house for
050         some reason. And it came in at a time when the other doctors'
051         from- Nancy used to support about five doctors, for about ten
052         years. She's been very ill over- she's very ill now. She has
053         Meniere's Disease and she fell over backwards in school (P) Friday-
054         Thursday or Friday and (...)
055   E                                           You mean the inner ear?
056   H                                                   Yeah inner ear
057         yeah. And she took a- just her- her feet gave out and she's been
058         in- in bed since- since then. Today's the first day- (...) Any-
059         how he called me up one day, (P) because I hadn't paid the bill.
060         And believe it or not when he *called* every other bill that had gotten
061         *in the way of his getting paid had been paid* and they're all cleared
062         out of the way but I was saving this big *monster*, the biggest one
063         of all, up so I could do a *frontal* assault on it when it- when
064         it came time to pay it. And I was sitting right where you are
065         and we had the phone here then. And he said Jim would it help
066         you at all if I considered- If I- he said if I reduced my bill.
067         Well I almost fell on the floor. Nobody had ever offered to do
068         that for me as long as I ever lived. (P) And I was so over-
069         *whelmed* that I- I was beset by- I had a very responsible job
070         and I- I come into a lot of money every- every day and I- I
071         worked for people who would absolutely crucify you if you made a
072         mistake. And ah- I was strung up all the time, really strung right
073         out. And when he said that to me I- I almost- I think I did get
074         a little bit dewy around the eyes, to think that anybody would
```

(Respondent continues)

```
075        have that much consideration who had, in particular, just done
076        such a terrific job on this kid. Everything came out beautiful.
077        And I said no, I wouldn't consider it, his reducing this bill at
078        all. I said I was about to call you up and here you are calling
079        me up on the telephone. And I said, believe it or not, you're
080        next up at bat. And I said I- you don't even know it, but 'n I-
081        I think I had kept him waiting about four months to pay the bill.
082        'n I said Bill, if you can just hang in there I'll get your- I'll
083        mail a check in about three or four days and that will start a run
084        on this thing and we'll stamp the life out of it, and that's what
085        we did. But uh- But that- I got very close to him and uh- He
086        had three or four children and was very much a- an enlightened
087        man and his son was in the Marines in Viet Nam and his hands were
088        tied behind his back and he was forced to kneel (on the ground)
089        and they shot him through the head. And he never got over it. He
090        moved out of Northgate. He sold a magnificent home over in the
091        Adam's Pond area and took his family up to Vermont. He was a great
092        skier and he does all his fracture work with skiers up there now in
093        Vermont and it just- took the starch right out of him.
094   E                                                     (P) But I take
095        it- Part of the question is what- what would you count as a high
096        point or low point of your (...) and what's the meaning (...)?
097   H   Well that would be a low point.
```

question was intended as a screening question that would allow us to pursue a more intensive inquiry about these selected times. I have also discussed the difficulties we had in arriving at a clear and mutually understood definition of high and low points.

At first reading the respondent's story appears to be an effort to clarify his own initial response, that is, what he means by "troubling times" that weren't "real troubles" but "enforced lean times" (003–005). At least this is how the story begins—as an explanation with a concrete example. The respondent was "held back" by the absence of a "feeling of financial security" from doing things he wanted to do, such as buying a boat. But the story is then elaborated and complicated. It becomes a narrative of triumph over adversity while at the same time it presents the respondent as a person with a valid social identity, as a responsible man who pays all bills, including the "monster" doctor's bill, despite financial strain. But then there is a further twist to the plot and the story becomes a tragedy. The son of the benevolent, competent, and "enlightened" doctor is killed in Vietnam. The doctor sells his "magnificent" home, gives up his practice and his good life in Northgate, and moves elsewhere. The death of his son "took the starch right out of him."

Systematic methods of narrative analysis must resolve a variety of problems, many of them evident in this story. For example, is this one story with related subplots or a series of different stories? Interpretations will differ depending on how we view the separate episodes. In either case we wish to examine how the narrator connects the several parts together to provide a coherent and continuous account. If the main point of the first story is that even in the absence of financial security "we always *did* what we had to do some*how* we did it. We got through it" (011–012), then the different medical expenses are thematically connected events as sources of financial strain: the bills for Danny's surgery for burns (014, 047–048), increasing costs of childbirth (014–020), and bills for his wife's surgery (027–029) and her other chronic medical problems (050–052). On the other hand there are discontinuities in the story, as that between the initial introduction of Danny's burn and skin graft (012–014) and the later new beginning and development of the same story (029–032, 042–046). And of course this event leads into the main point announced earlier, "We got through it" (012), that is now brought full circle in the conclusion, "and that's what we did" (084–085).

Some suggestive evidence that the first story "ends" at that point is the disruption in fluency as the respondent begins the tragic account of the doctor and his son, "But uh- But that- I got very close to him and uh-" (085). This last section has the quality of an epilogue telling us the fate of one of the central figures in the story. At a deeper level of interpretation this epilogue may be closely related to one of the primary aims of the whole story, namely, the wish of the narrator to show himself as a responsible man who paid his debts and who, in implicit contrast to the doctor, did not allow the troubles and stresses of life to take "the starch right out of him."

These observations are not a substitute for analysis.[4] The principal and limited aim of this introductory section is to show how a response, even in answer to a direct question in a relatively structured interview, may take the form of an account that resembles what we would all intuitively recognize as "some kind of story." This respondent/narrator sets the scene for us, introduces characters and describes their actions, specifies events and their relations over time, explicates a significant conflict and its resolution, and tells us the point of the story. These are features of more formal narratives; they serve as criteria in the definition of other oral and written accounts as stories and have been topics for systematic analysis.

Further, in this special interview context my role as the interviewer in the production of the story is evident in two ways. First, I allow the respondent to continue at length without interruption, even though it did not seem to me at the time, or in the initial analysis, that his response was a relevant answer to the question. In this respect I was following a general rule for conversationalists alert to the fact that a story is being told; that is, they allow the speaker to "hold the floor" beyond the limits of a usual turn. (See Labov and Fanshel, 1977, p. 105.) Second, I am the audience to whom the respondent is presenting himself in a particular light.

For reasons already discussed we do not know how common such responses may be in standard survey interviews. Respondents' storytelling tendencies may be suppressed by interviewers' interruptions[5] and the pragmatic demands of time and revelance, or stories may go unrecorded by interviewers or discarded in the analysis as irrelevant digressions (as when I first deleted this passage from the transcript of this interview). I have also suggested certain problems in narrative analysis, such as the difficulty in specifying story boundaries and the different levels of interpretation that may be required to relate subplots to each other and to the general point of a story.

Any approach to narrative analysis must deal with the familiar triad of linguistic topics—syntax, semantics, and pragmatics, the basic issues of structure, meaning, and interactional con-text—but investigators vary in how they formulate these prob-lems and which of them they see as primary. For some investigators the central question is whether there exist typical and perhaps universal story structures, that is, a standard set of story units organized in systematic ways irrespective of content, analogous to the way grammatical elements are arranged into sentences. Others are interested in the "structure" of content, that is, in how talk about different topics develops over the course of an account so that separate episodes are linked to-gether into a coherent and meaningful story. Still others are interested in how the construction of a story is affected by the interactional setting in which it is produced. Because the varied approaches direct attention to questions such as these and make them strong topics of inquiry, they implicitly confirm the gen-eral proposition informing this discussion, namely, that telling stories is a significant way for individuals to give meaning to and express their understandings of their experiences.

In the next section I focus on studies of narratives as they occur in interviews. Three approaches developed specifically for the analysis of interview narratives will be examined in de-tail; they vary in techniques for eliciting narratives as well as in concepts and methods of analysis. Together they suggest a range of systematic ways in which such research may be pursued. This restriction to interview research is consistent with the primary aim of this book; I discuss in the Appendix studies of other types of narrative, such as folk tales, literary narratives, histor-ical accounts, and stories constructed for the experimental study of cognition, memory, and learning.

The Analysis of Interview Narratives

Many researchers find my critique of mainstream methods per-suasive and appreciate the potential significance of respondents' stories. Nonetheless they find it difficult to envisage an alterna-tive that would satisfy, in a reasonable though perhaps different way, the standard, scientific criteria of objectivity, reliability, and validity. They want to know where we go from here and they pose a series of difficult and legitimate questions: How do we begin? What are the features of a well-designed study? How can analyses be evaluated for their adequacy and their rigor? Can studies be replicated?

The remainder of this chapter is, in part, a preliminary response to such questions. My aim is to show that narrative accounts can be analyzed in systematic ways to generate meaningful and promising findings. At the same time we must recognize that we are at an early stage in the development of this approach. In contrast to survey research, a well-worn tradition with widely agreed upon rules and procedures, in narrative analysis we find much diversity; different investigations bear a general family resemblance to one another but differ in theoretical orientation, in types of research questions formulated, and in method.

I have suggested that the sense of assurance mainstream researchers derive from standardized procedures is largely illusory, because it is based on assumptions that do not correspond to the essential nature of an interview as a form of discourse. Investigators following new paths of narrative analysis cannot rely on standard methods. Their confidence in the value of this direction of research comes instead from a theoretical and methodological perspective that requires close attentiveness to what interviewers and respondents say to each other, and how they say it. Further, this requirement means that in developing their interpretations and theories narrative analysts do not have the option of "distancing" themselves from the phenomenon of the talk itself in the way that survey analysts distance themselves through research strategies such as the statistical analysis of coded data. Although they differ in their particulars, the three approaches discussed here share this general perspective; they focus on the meanings and functions of different features and modes of speech.

To relate and contrast these approaches to one another in a systematic way, and occasionally to refer to other relevant studies, I organize my discussion around a framework of linguistic functions borrowed from Halliday's systemic theory of grammar (1970, 1973; see also de Joia and Stenton, 1980).[6] Halliday defines three analytically distinct but interdependent functions, all simultaneously present in any stretch of talk: the textual, referring to how parts of the text are internally connected through various syntactic and semantic devices; the ideational, or referential meaning of what is said; and the interpersonal, referring to the role relationships between speakers that are realized in the talk. The order of presentation of different approaches reflects the degree to which they tend to emphasize one or another of these functions.

Structural Analysis and the Textual Function: Elicited Personal Narratives

Labov and Waletzsky (1967) appear to have been the first to apply methods of linguistic analysis to interview narratives. Their aim is to "present an analytical framework for the analysis of oral versions of personal experience in English" (p. 12). They refer to their analysis as "functional," that is, story units and their connections are interpreted as serving referential or evaluative functions, and focus on the "smallest unit of linguistic expression" through which the various narrative functions are realized, "primarily the clause" (p. 13). Although they frame their analysis in terms of referential and evaluative functions—respectively, how a story corresponds to the real world and the point intended by the narrator—their approach centers on how "units of linguistic expression" are connected to one another, principally through a relation of temporal order. For this reason I consider their work an example of a study directed primarily to an analysis of what Halliday calls the textual function.

Labov and Waletzky examine a series of fourteen narratives told by subjects ranging in age from preadolescence through late adulthood. Almost all of these stories drawn from a large sample of interviews from several studies, as well as further examples reported in later papers by Labov (1972b, 1982), are elicited by questions about the danger of death or fighting: "Were you ever in a situation where you were in serious danger of being killed, where you said to yourself—'This is it'?" "Were you ever in a fight with a guy bigger than you? [R: Yes] What happened?" (1972b, p. 354). Labov argues that these questions are effective for getting samples of natural, "vernacular" speech, despite some minimal effect of the interviewer as an outside observer, because the respondent "seems to undergo a partial reliving of that experience, and he is no longer free to monitor his own speech as he normally does in face-to-face interviews" (1972b, p. 355).

To Labov and Waletzky (1967, p. 20), "the fundamental question of narrative analysis appears to be this: how can we relate the sequence of clauses in the narrative to the sequence of events inferred from the narrative?" Their answer lies in their definition of narrative "as one method of recapitulating past experience by matching a verbal sequence of clauses to the sequence of events which actually occurred." Labov and Waletzky distinguish such accounts from other forms of reporting or recapitulating experience, such as an alternative account of the same events, an identical set of clauses arranged in a different order, even where the latter conveys the same meaning and is an equally and "perfectly logical, orderly, and acceptable" representation of the sequence of events. Their criterion is reality congruence, and it represents a particular model of the relation between language and reality. It is in terms of this underlying model that they can assert that the specification of temporal ordering as the "fundamental question" "proceeds" from the referential function of narratives.

Temporal ordering is a central problem in narrative analysis; as we shall see later, other investigators approach it differently. Labov applies this definition of narrative with rigor and consistency. He defines a "minimal narrative" as "a sequence of two clauses which are *temporally ordered:* that is, a change in their order will result in a change in the temporal sequence of the original semantic interpretation" (1972b, p. 360). The immediate and obvious problem is that respondents' narrative accounts include much more than a sequence of temporally ordered clauses. Not only may narratives be expanded through, for example, successive chaining of minimal narratives with each next clause answering the question, And what happened next?, but much more may be included in the narrative besides pairs of temporally ordered clauses; this is clearly evident in the interview excerpt presented earlier in Transcript 4.

In large part the technical apparatus Labov and Waletzky develop and apply to "narratives of personal experience" is directed to answering questions engendered by this problem, such as: How can we determine whether an account is a narrative or another form of "recapitulating" experience? How can we isolate the essential "narrative structure" from the flow of talk? What functions can we ascribe to other, nonnarrative parts of the account? How do groups and individuals differ in the ways they construct narratives, for example, in their complexity?

The key to this type of analysis is the definition of a narrative clause. This is the fundamental unit. It is defined as a clause that cannot be moved or relocated to any other point in the account without a change in its "semantic interpretation." The range of possible movement without such a change in meaning is called a "displacement range." Analysis proceeds by testing each clause "for the potential range of displacement by examining the semantic interpretation that results when the clause in question is moved to all possible positions in the remaining sequence" (Labov and Waletzky, 1967, p. 22). A clause that has no freedom of movement is "locked in position in the sequence; it evidently functions as a *narrative clause* of the simplest kind, maintaining the strict temporal sequence that is the defining characteristic of narrative." The polar opposite of a narrative clause is a "free" clause that "has a displacement set equal to the entire narrative, and can range freely through the narrative sequence." Two other types of clauses are distinguished: coordinate clauses that have "identical displacement sets . . . and may be freely interchanged without any change in temporal sequence" and restricted clauses that may be displaced in one direction or the other but do not have the range of free clauses.

One of Labov's (1972b, p. 361) examples of a minimal narrative indicates how these types of clauses differ from one another:

a   I know a boy named Harry.
b   Another boy threw a bottle at him right in the head
c   and he had to get seven stitches.

Clauses *b* and *c* are narrative clauses temporally related to each other, but *a* is a free clause because it "might be placed after *b* or *c* without disturbing temporal order."

These and other clauses may be classified into one or another of the six categories of a fully formed narrative: Abstract, Orientation, Complicating Action, Evaluation, Result or Resolution, and Coda. Complicating Action is the narrative itself and is constituted by narrative clauses. In a minimal narrative the only element is the Complicating Action, but a narrative serving only the referential function is "abnormal: it may be considered empty or pointless narrative" (Labov and Waletzky, 1967, p. 13). An Abstract, where the narrator begins by summarizing the story; an Orientation, where time, place, and persons are identified; a Resolution, stating the result of the action; or a Coda, which returns the speakers to the present situation—all of these are optional and their absence does not detract from the interest or pointfulness of the narrative. The latter, however, depends on Evaluation, that is, "the means used by the narrator to indicate the point of the narrative, its raison d'être: why it was told, and what the narrator is getting at" (1972b, p. 366).

Typically the elements of a complete narrative are sequentially ordered, from Abstract to Coda, but this is not a strong restriction; clauses signifying Orientation or Evaluation may appear at various points. The narrative role of Evaluation is of particular importance and Labov, noting its neglect in other studies of narratives, devotes most of his 1972 paper to various types of evaluative devices and to a comparison of their uses by different types of speakers. Speakers may, for example, suspend the flow of narrative action by comments on how they felt about what was going on, or they may dramatize the action. Evaluation may also be realized linguistically through alteration of the simple and straightforward syntax of the narrative clause. Labov illustrates several syntactic devices, such as intensifiers, by which an event in the narrative is selected for emphasis, or comparators, by which actual events are compared to events that did not occur; various other types of qualification and explication serve an evaluative purpose. As an indication of the usefulness of this scheme, Labov reports, in a study of the narratives of preadolescents, adolescents, and adults, "a regular and marked increase" (1972b, p. 394) with age in the use of all the main categories of evaluative syntactic devices.

It is of some interest that Labov's distinction between Complicating Action and Evaluation as components of narrative, and his emphasis on the latter, closely parallels the view of the literary critics Scholes and Kellogg (1966). Although they are not concerned with matching the temporal ordering of events in the real world with those in a story, their definition of plot is similar to Labov's definition of narrative structure: "Plot is, in every sense of the word, the articulation of the skeleton of narrative" (p. 12), and "Plot can be defined as the dynamic, sequential element in narrative literature" (p. 207). Perhaps of more significance, in its relation to Labov's focus on Evaluation, is their observation on other aspects of narrative: "What we respond to in the greatest narratives is the quality of mind transmitted to us through the language of characterization, motivation, description, and commentary . . . Quality of mind . . . not plot, is the soul of narrative. Plot is only the indispensable skeleton which, fleshed out with character and incident, provides the necessary clay into which life may be breathed" (p. 239).

I have several reasons for beginning this review of narrative analysis with Labov and Waletzky. As I mentioned earlier, their paper appears to be the first systematic attempt to study narratives occurring in interviews. Second, their work is restricted to one type of narrative with a relatively simple structure and focuses primarily on only one of Halliday's discourse functions, the textual. Their model serves as an introduction to other approaches that address more complex narratives and explore additional functions. Further, their method may be more accessible to other interview researchers than those to which I will shortly turn, because the mode of analysis bears a close resemblance to the use of code-category systems in survey interview research. The elements of a fully formed narrative, from Abstract to Coda, and the different types of evaluative devices provide a set of codes for classifying the "narrative functions" of different parts of the account; definitions of these categories are equivalent to a coding manual. Results of such an analysis can be counted, tabulated, and compared across groups according to the familiar procedures of statistical analysis, as Labov himself had done (1972b). Finally, this work is widely cited and has influenced other investigators.

On the other hand some problems with this approach merit attention. Although this is not the place for a detailed critical analysis, given that the principal aim here is expository, brief comment on two central issues may help us appreciate the significance and implications of different approaches. There are two fundamental questions all students of interview narratives must address: What are the effects on the production of a narrative, the respondent's "story," of the interview as a particular context and of the interviewer as questioner, listener, and coparticipant in the discourse? And how should one take into account, in theory and analysis, relations between events in the real world and these events expressed in the narrative, such as their respective temporal orderings, their modes of connection and forms of organization, and their functional significance? Respectively, these questions refer to Halliday's interpersonal and ideational functions.

Regarding the first question, I believe that effects of the interviewer and the interview context are seriously underestimated in their work. Labov's notion that respondents appear to be partially "reliving" their experience when they tell stories about dramatic and stressful events in their lives and therefore do not "monitor" their talk is neither reasonable in terms of our general understanding of discourse nor in accord with what we know of the interview process. As I have noted at various points, and as I will show in more detail below, the interviewer's presence and form of involvement—how she or he listens, attends, encourages, interrupts, digresses, initiates topics, and terminates responses—is integral to a respondent's account. It is in this specific sense that a "story" is a joint production. How the interviewer's role is to be taken into account is of course a difficult problem, but it is not solved by making the interviewer invisible and inaudible, by painting her or him out of the picture.[7]

Labov and Waletzky's answer to the second question is clear and unequivocal: a narrative is a distinctive type of "recapitulation" of experience that preserves the temporal ordering of events in the real world. They apply this definition rigorously by specifying the temporal "displacement ranges" of clauses and isolating the narrative proper, that is, the sequence of narrative clauses, from the respondent's full account. Nonetheless, despite the rigor and the degree of attention to temporal ordering, there is a puzzling consequence of the definition. Stated briefly, the narrative itself, consisting in the sequence of temporally ordered narrative clauses and constituting the category of Complicating Action in the full framework, turns out to be relatively uninteresting. In Labov's first empirical application of the model (1972b), analyses are directed primarily to the Evaluation component, those parts of the account that make up the point of the story. Evaluative clauses are "free" and have no required connection to the temporal ordering of events; they may appear at any place in the narrative account. Labov isolates the narrative sections of respondents' answers to his questions, but these sections are put aside when he turns to actual analyses of data. His analysis focuses on the differential use of evaluative strategies and devices among individuals of different age and ethnic groups.[8]

This apparent paradox in the Labov-Waletzky model, the theoretical importance attached to temporal ordering accompanied by its relative neglect in empirical analyses, is resolved in a particular way in a recent paper by Labov (1982). Focusing on narratives of unexpected violent action, Labov addresses the question, "How then, can narratives of personal experience be used to illuminate relations of speech and action in the world reported by narrative?" (p. 220). Note that the relation between speech and action is no longer to be captured simply by matching their respective temporal orderings; this relation now must be "illuminated" through the study of personal narratives.

Using an "approach to speech acts as forms of action" (p. 224) and the framework developed in Labov and Fanshel (1977) for the analysis of rules for speech acts, particularly the Rule of Requests, Labov argues that the cohesion of narratives "does not depend on the sequence of narrative clauses but on the sequences of speech acts and actions that the narrative presents" (p. 233). That is, analysis is focused on the social functions of acts and events in the real world as these are expressed in the narrative account.

This new approach seems like a major change in how the model is to be understood and applied, and Labov notes important differences between this and his earlier "descriptive" studies: "Much of the attention of previous analyses has focused on the elaboration of narrative beyond the fundamental sequence of narrative clauses. The main thrust of this discussion is in the other direction: to reduce the narrative to its skeletal outline of narrative clauses, and to outline the generating mechanism that produces the narrative backbone" (p. 227). The change in direction is accomplished by moving to a higher level of abstraction, that is, by characterizing the narrative clauses in terms of the social meanings of the events they report. Thus, after outlining the narrative structures of his illustrative cases, Labov remarks: "It would seem therefore that the construction of an objective event sequence has not so far advanced our understanding of the violent reactions in these narratives. The sense of strangeness remains: these people did not behave as we expect people to behave. This effect is not due to the transformation of the narrative through the insertion of interpretative or evaluative material, but seems inherent in the events themselves" (p. 232).

Introducing Goffman's concept of a Move, defined as "an interaction that alters or threatens to alter the relative social positions of the interactants" (p. 242), and combining it with a consideration of the ways that requests and responses to requests may function to confirm or threaten social status, Labov arrives at a highly abstract transformation or rewriting of the original narratives. For example, the twenty-nine clauses of one of the original accounts, first transformed into a narrative structure of nine temporally ordered clauses with an Orientation, are restated as three Moves that lead to violent action. In the end Labov explains the violent act as a consequence of denial by one person of another's legitimate right to make a request; the re-jection threatens the social status of the requester and leads to the violent reaction.

Labov's modification of his earlier model aligns his work more closely with the tradition of functional analysis. This tradition begins with Propp's (1928) study of Russian fairy tales. The key to Propp's analysis lies in his specification of functions as basic components of stories and his explicit requirement that functions be defined only in the context of the full story, because the same action (or event) may have different functions or meanings and different actions may serve the same function. He asserts that "the functions of the dramatis personae are basic components of the tale, and we must first of all extract them . . . Secondly, an action cannot be defined apart from its place in the course of narration. The meaning which a given function has in the course of action must be considered . . . Thus, identical acts can have different meanings, and vice versa. *Function is understood as an act of a character, defined from the point of view of its significance for the course of action*" (p. 21). The strength of Propp's analysis comes from his demonstration that "*all fairy tales are of one type in regard to their structure*" (p. 23) and that "*the sequence of functions is always identical*" (p. 22). Propp develops a list of thirty-one separate functions, for example: "The villain causes harm or injury to a member of a family"; "The hero is approached with a request or command"; "The hero is tested"; "The hero acquires the use of a magical agent"; "The villain is punished"; "The hero is married and ascends the throne" (pp. 25–65).

Fairy-tale functions are somewhat esoteric, and the power and potential value of Propp's analysis for other types of narratives may not be readily apparent. Landau's (1984) elegant and lucid analysis of evolutionary theories as narratives is highly suggestive of how the approach may be applied to other data. Landau examines six "narratives of human evolution," Darwin's and the theories of five other scientists at the beginning of the twentieth century. She observes that each of them recognized the same four events as major episodes in human evolution: "a shift from the trees to the ground (terrestriality), the development of upright posture (bipedalism), the development of the brain, intelligence, and language (encephalization), and the development of technology, morals, and society (civilization) . . . Which episode came first has been an important source of debate; in fact each of the five authors under discussion here proposes a different sequence" (p. 264). The original Labov-Waletzky model, with its emphasis on matching narrative clauses and events, would discourage any effort at comparative analysis of these theories in view of this disagreement about the temporal ordering of significant events. Using Propp's approach, Landau discerns that the different theorists "seem to have in mind a similar narrative pattern, which, for present purposes, can be represented in terms of nine functions." These functions refer to the "journey" of a "hero," namely, the human ancestor, from an original state of equilibrium, through a series of "tests," to the "achievement of humanity [which] may be thought to signify the hero's final triumph" (p. 264), the triumph being his transformation into civilized modern man by special "gifts," such as tools, reason, or a moral sense. For the different theorists, the same function is served by different events; for example, either encephalization or bipedalism may mark the shift from the initial state; either terrestriality or bipedalism may serve as the event initiating the next stage of the journey. (For a detailed analysis of one theorist's narrative, see Landau, 1986.)

The linkage suggested here between Labov's "functional" modification of his earlier model and the Proppian tradition marks an important convergence. The limited usefulness for analysis of Labov and Waletzky's initial formulation of temporal ordering derives from the concrete equivalence or "identity" that they require between a narrative clause and an actual event. Labov's abstract reformulation of reported events as Moves and requests allows for the analysis of functional meanings in a way similar to that of Propp and Landau. Labov still relies directly on a description of the "objective event sequence" to provide the narrative "skeleton" for analysis. I do not think this will turn out to be a critical feature of functional analyses. If Propp's emphasis on context is recognized as necessary to the interpretation of meaning (see also Mishler, 1979) and the function of an act or event is "defined from the point of view of its significance for the course of action," then functional analysis will depend not on the surface similarity between a narrative clause and a real event but on the way the former functions in the overall narrative as a representation or reconstruction of the real world, much as in Landau's analysis.

Labov's new work is clearly referential, thus incorporating Halliday's ideational function, and thereby serves as a bridge to another approach, to which I now turn.

Coherence and the Ideational Function: Life-History Narratives

A second line of narrative research focuses on the organization of accounts in terms of "coherence." A narrator's intentions and narrative strategies used to produce a coherent story are central topics of inquiry. Referential meaning—that is, content—expressed through "themes" and their relations to each other is fundamental to analysis and interpretation. Looking at coherence in a narrative suggests how, in Halliday's terms, the ideational function may be related to the textual function.

Combining their respective interests in thematic analysis of ethnographic materials (Agar, 1979, 1980) and discourse analysis drawn from work in artificial intelligence (AI) (Hobbs, 1978; Hobbs and Robinson, 1979), Agar and Hobbs (1982, p. 1) propose to use "AI formalisms as a formal language of description for the complex conversational behavior that occurs in ethnographic interviews" (see also Agar and Hobbs, 1983, and Hobbs and Agar, 1981). They note that life-history interviews present persistent and stubborn problems for anthropological analysis: "it remains true that the more the informal interview is controlled by the informant, the less the ethnographer knows how to deal with it . . . there is little sense of what to do with such material beyond fairly straightforward presentations of the interview as narrated by the informant . . . life histories are valued for their person-centered, holistic displays of principles otherwise discussed more abstractly in ethnographies, but there is not much discussion of how to make those links explicit" (Agar and Hobbs, 1982, pp. 2–3). Their comments apply as well to problems encountered by psychologists, sociologists, oral historians, and other social scientists who rely on extended and open-ended interview responses for their data. Agar and Hobbs offer a systematic method for the analysis of such materials.

The central idea in the Agar-Hobbs model is "coherence." Hobbs (1978, p. 5) defines this term as follows: "I will call a discourse 'coherent' if it exhibits structural relationships between its various segments, which depend on the propositional content of the segments." Attempting to give *coherence* a "technical" and precise meaning, he distinguishes it from such related terms as *cohesion, relevance,* and *understandability* and from other definitions of the word, such as that presenting coherence as talk about the same "topic." In contrast to those who would treat coherence as primarily a function of general syntactic or semantic features of utterances or sentences (for example, Halliday and Hasan, 1976), Hobbs focuses on the on-line problems faced by people in conversation to achieve a shared sense of their talk as being tied together.

Noting that the "fundamental question in an investigation of coherence" arises from the fact that discourses tend to be longer than single clauses, Hobbs argues that the intuitive sense of a text or discourse as coherent reflects the operation of a specific set of relations between its parts that may be inferred by speakers and listeners—and by investigators as well. These are "coherence relations." "Coherence in discourse can be characterized by means of a small number of *coherence relations* which are definable in terms of the operations of an inference system. If an utterance strikes one intuitively as a coherent continuation of the discourse there is some coherence relation that holds between the utterance and some portion of the preceding discourse. If it strikes one as incoherent, no such relation exists" (Hobbs, 1978, p. 3).

Hobbs specifies a number of such relations, each framed by and directed to answering the question, "what needs to get done in discourse that would lead us to say that a series of utterances constitutes a single discourse rather than a sequence of contiguous discourses?" (p. 12). Taken together, these provide a taxonomy of coherence relations and include devices such as weak causal and strong temporal relations between events, evaluations of the appropriateness or effectiveness of an utterance in terms of the overall goal of the discourse, linkages between what is known and what is introduced as new information, and various types of expansion and elaboration. These are the ways that participants do the "work" that produces their sense of a cohesive discourse; they are also the analytic categories an investigator uses to interpret a series of utterances as coherent. The model allows "that all discourse is not coherent . . . in casual conversational situations, we typically find islands of coherence of varying sizes with more or less successful attempts to bridge between them" (p. 8).

Agar and Hobbs (1982) further elaborate this model in analyzing a fragment from a life-history interview with a heroin addict. They specify three general types of coherence, each imparting its own particular form of unity to the text. All three are included in their microanalysis of the addict's story, and the narrative structure of the story is described in terms of each type. The three types are (a) global coherence, or how a particular utterance is related to a speaker's overall plan, intent, or goal for the conversation; (b) local coherence, which refers more narrowly to relations between utterances and parts of the text and is specified primarily through Hobb's taxonomy of coherence relations; and (c) themal coherence, or how utterances express a speaker's recurrent assumptions, beliefs, and goals, or "cognitive world." Distinguishing between local and global coherence, Agar and Hobbs (1982, p. 7) state that global coherence provides a "top-down view" and local coherence a "bottom-up view." "The requirements of global coherence say, 'Given the overall goals I am trying to accomplish, what can I say next that will serve them?' Local coherence says, "Given what I just said, what can I say that is related to it?' "

The aim and product "of the microanalysis is simultaneously an explication of the text and a presentation of a specific portion of the speaker's cognitive world, that part which the formal

theory of coherence has forced us to assume if we are to explicate the text" (p. 9). The way this model works may be illustrated by their analysis of the opening utterances in the first
episode of a respondent's story about how he became a burglar.
This episode, beginning about eleven minutes into the interview, marks a shift from background material to his narration
of events leading up to his meeting with a "fence," someone who
would buy stolen property (p. 12):

(1.1)   J: And one Sunday morning about ohhhh five o'clock in
the morning
(1.2)   I sat down in the Grand-
(1.3)   no, no, not in the Grand Central, in the Penn Station,
(1.4)   and while I was sitting there a young cat came up to
me,
(1.5)   and he had his *duffel* bag and a suitcase,
(1.6)   and he said, "Look," he said, "maaan," he said, "I've got
to make the john.
(1.7)   Will you keep your *eye* on the—on my stuff for me?"

Agar and Hobbs assert that the complete episode has a structure found in many narratives, including specification of a setting (1.1–1.3), presentation of a problem (1.4–1.7), and, as the
narrator continues with his story, consideration of a first alternative plan of action, intervening circumstances, the choice of a
second alternative action, and an outcome. In the first step of
their structural analysis, they show how these components are
linked together through various coherence devices; this is local
coherence. For example, setting and problem utterances are
related to each other through a subtype of the linkage coherence relation, namely, providing a description of the setting as
background to the action. The second alternative line of action
expressed later in the story, that is, actually stealing the bags, is
linked by the coherence relation of explanation to the circum-
stance that there are two eyewitnesses to the scene who propose
stealing the bags and splitting what is found.

Further detailed examination of how the other types of coherence are manifested in the text enriches our understanding
of how the story and the way it is told express the structure and
content of the respondent's cognitive world. For example, Agar

and Hobbs note that because a time theme is a recurrent motif in the interviews the first utterance (1.1) displays themal coherence. The specification of "one Sunday morning about ohhhh five o'clock in the morning" emphasizes another related, recurrent theme, the difference between the straight and addict worlds, the latter involving settings with around-the-clock availability, any day of the week, for activities. However, Agar and Hobbs point out that this specification of an exact time is inconsistent with the respondent's usual representation of the time theme which stresses the unimportance of chronological time and of the clock and calendar in street life. This difference and the consequent violation of the interviewer's usual expectations signal a shift in the organization and overall goal of the account from background description to narration of the story itself; thus the statement exhibits global coherence.

Agar and Hobbs summarize the result of their analysis of this first utterance: "The utterance is locally coherent, playing a well-defined function in the story of Episode One. It shows a global coherence by signaling a shift in the overall organization of the interview as a whole. It also shows themal coherence, tying in with various other portions of this and other interviews in the way it makes use of facts about Jack's world and in the role it plays in the situation of a straight listening to a story by a junkie" (p. 14).

Agar and Hobbs's multilevel analysis specifying three types of coherence preserves some of the complexity and richness of a narrative account; at the same time it suggests a methodic way of relating form and content. As I indicated in discussing Labov's work, placing primary emphasis on one problem may be associated with the neglect of others. Although the strength of the Agar-Hobbs model lies in the analysis of coherence—different types at different levels with different functions—the treatment of other issues that must be addressed by narrative analysis is lacking in this model.

These issues may be stated as a series of questions; comparing other approaches with Agar and Hobbs's answers will help clarify certain problems in narrative analysis and suggest alternative paths to their resolution. First, what is the relationship between levels of analysis? In the Agar-Hobbs model the issue is one of levels of coherence. Second, do narratives or stories have a particular structure that distinguishes them from other types of accounts? If such a structure is postulated, how does it enter into the analysis? Third, what is the basis for interpreting the meaning of an account? That is, what assumptions does an analyst rely on in making inferences about a narrator's intention? Finally, what are the effects of context on the narrative account? In terms of our special interests, how is the narrative influenced by the interview situation and what role does the interviewer play in its production?

Agar and Hobbs's answers to these questions are clear but unexplicated; they remain largely implicit in their analyses. First, the investigators do not specify any particular form of relationship between the three types or levels of coherence. Although all are included in a full-stage microanalysis, each is analyzed by itself. The form of coherence found at one level does not inform or constrain coherence at other levels; the three levels are independent of one another and require different interpretive models and analytic procedures. Second, Agar and Hobbs do not specify any general type of narrative structure, nor do they define narratives in ways that would mark them as different from other types of accounts or texts. Although they refer in passing to typical narratives as having a setting, problem, plan of action, and outcome, these categories do not enter into their analysis.

In arriving at an understanding of this respondent's account, Agar and Hobbs infer aims, intentions, motives, and values on the basis of both their general knowledge as members of the larger culture and their special knowledge of the addict's world acquired from ethnographic study and other interviews. (See Agar, 1979, 1980.) Their interpretation of themal and global coherence in the respondent's references to the time of events depends on both their general and special domains of knowledge. They do not provide rules or guidelines for making such inferences; in this specific sense their interpretive procedure is not systematic. They ground their interpretations in their commonsense understanding and general stock of knowledge and rely on unstated or silent assumptions about reasonableness, relevance, and appropriateness in making sense of the account.

Although aware of the special nature of an interview as an interactive context, Agar and Hobbs treat the account as though it belongs essentially to the respondent. They note that the text is "for all purposes a monologue, since the interviewer participates only through minimal back channeling signals" (1982, p. 5). They recognize that the respondent is aware of the interviewer's presence and perspective, for example, when they interpret the respondent's specification of exact time as a violation of interviewer expectations and thus as a marker of global coherence, but the interviewer is not viewed as an active coparticipant in the production of the story.

These observations are not intended as criticisms in the narrow sense of the term. All investigators have to make choices and those made by Agar and Hobbs enlarge our understanding of the complexity of interview narratives and show how an analysis can both respect the particularities of an account and relate an individual's story to general cultural themes and values. My intent here is to take note of certain issues by examining the assumptions and consequences of the choices.

The implications of different choices are quite evident when we compare Agar and Hobbs's treatment of these questions with that of another approach to the problem of coherence, one that in some respects bears a resemblance to theirs but in other respects differs in significant ways.[9] This is the comprehensive "general discourse processing model" developed by van Dijk (1977, 1980, 1982, 1983; see also Kintsch, 1977). The resemblances are apparent in van Dijk's distinctions among levels of discourse—he specifies microstructures, macrostructures, and superstructures, or cultural schemata; in his description of production and comprehension as involving both "top-down" strategies using "global" frameworks and meanings and "bottom-up" strategies that depend on particular features and "signals" in the actual discourse; and in his emphasis on culturally and contextually grounded "scripts," "frames," "schemata," "themes," and "propositions."

Differences between the two models are equally apparent. First, van Dijk specifies a systematic relationship between levels, namely, a hierarchical one. The macrostructure with its constituent macropropositions is derived from the microstructure through a series of macrorules, such as deletion and generalization, "that map microstructures onto macrostructures" (1980, p. 51). In this way the particular features and meanings of actual discourse are transformed into a more general and more abstract "type" of discourse, and the former is interpreted as an instance of the latter.

In addition, narrative is only one of several types of superstructures van Dijk considers; others he examines include arguments, research reports, and advertisements. The type of superstructure represented by specific texts enters into production-comprehension-interpretive processes:

> Readers/hearers of natural stories have both schematic and thematic contextual expectations about discourse genre (story) and topics (global contents) that act top-down, strategically, to monitor the on-line process of understanding . . . propositions and proposition sequences are construed strategically (on-line) according to (i) general constraints on coherence, and (ii) in particular with reference to possible action structures (for our culture) . . . Whereas local clause and sentence interpretation already provide many cues about the discourse genre, and hence about possible schemata, the actual overall narrative structure can only be inferred (construed) at the global level of comprehension . . . in a mixed strategic (top-down and bottom-up) process, macropropositions are assigned to possible narrative categories, that is, they are *functionally* interpreted . . . The specific narrative constraints on the (global) semantics of the story will be culturally variable.   (1983, p. 599)

The difference between the Agar-Hobbs and van Dijk models are striking with respect to how the nature and function of narratives is defined and what relationships between levels are specified. I find it more difficult to determine how they differ in the ways that the investigators, as analysts, arrive at an understanding of the "meaning" of a story. As might be expected from this brief description of his model, van Dijk develops a highly elaborated system of categories that he then applies to the analysis of "macrostructures . . . as semantic global structures in discourse" (1980, p. 27). Nonetheless, based on my review of his analyses of various texts, my impression is that he relies fundamentally, in the same way that Agar and Hobbs do, on his general knowledge of culturally shared meanings. The extended and detailed presentation of his model, in *Macrostructures* (1980), is peppered with frequent metacomments on his own analysis as "informal," "semisystematic," "semi-intuitive," "partially intuitive." He says that the characterization of different texts as representative of particular macrostructures or superstructures, a specification that plays a significant role in analysis, is "socioculturally determined," dependent on "conventions," "stereotypes," and "well-known social frames." I believe that van Dijk's observations about how he does the actual work of analysis are accurate.

What are we to make of this finding that two approaches, differing markedly in general form and specific detail, both rely in the end for their interpretations of meaning on the intuitive grounds of shared cultural understandings? My own view is that the use of cultural understandings is unavoidable and that analyses of naturally occurring discourse, such as interview narratives, require that the investigator "add to" or supplement the text through a step that Labov and Fanshel (1977, p. 49) refer to as "expansion." In this process the analyst brings "together all the information that we have that will help in understanding the production, interpretation, and sequencing of the utterance in question." To accomplish this expansion of meaning, the analyst uses her or his "best understanding," makes explicit pronomial or elliptical references to other material as well as to presumably shared knowledge between the participants, and introduces factual material from other parts of the interview or from general knowledge of the world. Labov and Fanshel provide such expansions on an utterance-by-utterance basis; the process is more implicit in the Agar-Hobbs and van Dijk analyses.

Contextual issues, that is, the effects of the interview situation and the role of the interviewer, are not addressed systematically by either Agar and Hobbs or van Dijk. Although both models extend the scope of narrative analysis to include Halliday's ideational and textual functions, the interpersonal function does not receive serious consideration. In the following section an approach is described that addresses the problem of how a respondent's stories may be shaped by the interviewer-interviewee relationship.

Interview Contexts and the Interpersonal Function: Narratives in Focused Interviews

I have already remarked the general neglect among interview-narrative researchers of effects on respondents' stories of the special contexts of interviews. In this respect their work has not advanced our understanding much beyond that of mainstream survey researchers. Within the perspective developed here, with interviews conceptualized as jointly produced discourses, certain questions take on particular significance and require analysis. For example, what is the role of the interviewer in how a respondent's story is told, how it is constructed and developed, and what it means? In particular, how do an interviewer's questions, assessments, silences, and responses enter into a story's production? How do stories told in interviews differ from those told in other contexts, such as naturally occurring conversations? Do different types of interview and question formats produce different types of stories? How can the presence and influence of an interviewer be taken into account in the analysis and interpretation of a respondent's story?

Paget's work is a notable exception to the general neglect of issues involved in an interviewer's participation in a story's production. In her analyses of interviews she conducted with physicians (1982, 1983b) and with artists (1983a), her presence as the interviewer is explicitly recognized. In reporting an interview with a woman artist, Paget states that she is concerned with the "dynamic structure of in-depth interviews" (1983a, p. 79) and that her aim is to "explore in-depth interviewing as a science of subjective experience" (p. 67). Her approach combines detailed description of linguistic features of spoken discourse with the hermeneutic tradition of interpretation. Her mode of interviewing is intended to encourage the respondent's speech and give her as much control as possible over pacing and the introduction and development of content. Contrasting this approach with survey interviewing, Paget notes that the distinctive feature of in-depth interviewing is "that the answers given continually inform the evolving conversation" (p. 78), and she grounds her analysis of relations between questions and replies in the "dialectic of the interview" (p. 80).

Paget points out that her questions presume neither neutrality nor objectivity on her part, but reveal her personal interest in her subject's art as well as in her own research project, which is to understand creative work in contemporary society. Reflectively examining the form and quality of her questions, which were not standardized and predetermined by an interview schedule, she observes that they often have a hesitant and halting quality as she searches for ways to ask about what she wants to learn; they are formulated and reformulated over the course of the interview. She suggests that this way of questioning may allow for and encourage replies that are equally searching, hesitant, and formulated in the process of answering; that is, she creates a situation where the respondent too is engaged in a search for understanding. Paget refers also to the significance of her silences for how her respondent comes to tell her story in her own way, noting that at many points, for example, when the respondent paused, she remained silent when she "might have entered the stream of speech" (p. 77).

Paget's general interest in creativity and the making of works of art is specified in terms of a series of topics that she asks about in the interviews: how the artist's work developed, training, other types of work done, preparation for and showing of work. Her view of her respondent's account as a story draws in part on Labov's model, and she refers both to the story's plot as action through time and to comments on the action expressing the speaker's attitude that Labov would label the Evaluative component.

To illustrate her approach, Paget reports an exchange where the respondent answers what appears on the surface to be a simple, direct question with a lengthy, complex account; this type of reply is similar to the expanded response to a direct question in the interview excerpt with which this chapter began. The interviewer has asked the respondent's age at the time discussed earlier in the interview when the respondent "first" became serious about being an artist. Paget discusses the apparent "disparity" between question and response. Although the respondent begins with a direct answer stating her current age and estimating her age at the earlier time, she then continues and her full response "overwhelms the question" (p. 81). Among other topics the artist refers to her feelings of competitiveness with her mother, who was an artist, how she started to paint after her mother died, how she felt when she sold some of her mother's possessions and jewelry in order to buy paint.

Paget argues that her question about the respondent's age and the extended reply cannot be understood if the question is viewed as identical in meaning to the typical age question in the list of social-background items appearing at the end of a standard survey interview schedule. Her question is embedded in and enters into the evolving discourse of the interview. To analyze its meaning and the meaning of the response, the question-answer exchange "cannot be severed from shared historical understandings" (p. 79). Reviewing her own experiences and thoughts during the interview, Paget reflects on how the question emerged from her own wondering at that point, given what she had already learned about the artist's life, about whether she and her respondent were "contemporaries" and had shared in the political events and experiences of that earlier time: "I wondered if she too was from the sixties" (p. 82). Paget's view of interviews as jointly produced discourses in which the interviewer is "always implicated in the construction of the phenomena analyzed" (p. 78) informs all aspects of her work: her mode of interviewing, her relationship to her respondents, her method of transcription, and her analysis and interpretation.

It is evident from examples used in this chapter that narratives may occur in response to closed as well as open-ended questions, that they may be elicited by direct questions about experiences assumed to be common if not universal, such as a fight or a violent confrontation with death, that they may be the form through which respondents talk about their lives in ethnographic oral-history interviews or in in-depth interviews about the development of their work. By referring to focused-interview narratives in the heading to this section, I wished to indicate somewhat more specifically the range of interview settings in which narratives have been found and studied. I borrowed the term from the well-known manual for focused interviews by Merton, Fiske, and Kendall (1956). This form of interview is designed to study variation in perceptions and responses of individuals who have been exposed to the same event or been involved in the same situation. Merton, Fiske, and Kendall refer to "a distinctive prerequisite of the focused interview" being a "prior analysis of the situation in which subjects have been involved" (p. 4). Among the criteria they list for effective and productive focused interviews, in addition to encouragement of specific reports to a wide range of stimulus elements in the original situation, are "*Depth*. The interview should help interviewees to describe the affective, cognitive and evaluative meanings of the situation and the degree of their involvement in it"; and "*Personal context*. The interview should bring out the attributes and prior experience of interviewees which endow the situation with these distinctive meanings" (p. 12).

Paget's approach blends qualities of life-history and focused interviewing. Her inquiry encompasses much more of a person's life than a narrowly specified particular situation experienced by all her respondents. Nonetheless her attention is centered, or focused, primarily on a general "situation" that they have in common, namely, the conditions and consequences of their work as artists. Bell's (1983) interviews of DES daughters somewhat more closely resemble the focused-interview model. All her subjects had in common their exposure in utero to DES; recent research has shown that DES daughters are at higher than normal risk of "vaginal and cervical cancer, problem pregnancies, and possible infertility" (p. 7).[10]

Bell's aim is to understand how DES daughters perceive, understand, and cope with these risks. From her "prior analysis of the situation" she developed a list of topics to be covered, including how her respondents first learned of their exposure, how their experiences changed over time and how they envision the future, their medical problems and their experiences with and management of medical care, and their relationships with husbands, mothers, other family members, and friends, as well as effects on their work and social lives. Her mode of inquiry also followed the general lines of in-depth interviewing that encourages respondents to "guide the flow of talk and to provide coherence in the interview" (p. 7).

Bell combines and adapts the story-grammar and narrative-structure approaches developed, respectively, by cognitive psychologists and by ethnographers and sociolinguists.[11] She focuses on three problems that become apparent in in-depth interviews but have received little attention in these traditions of story analysis. These are: relations among episodes within stories; relations between stories in the same interview; and effects on story structure and development of the dual and shifting roles of interviewee and interviewer, the former as both narrator and respondent and the latter as listener and questioner. Bell's key assumption is that interview narratives are grounded in the interplay between these dual roles.

One of her concerns is how to define beginnings and endings, that is, the boundaries, of episodes and stories and the ways they are tied together and related to each other. Bell offers a preliminary analysis of a story having four linked episodes. About fifteen minutes into the interview, her respondent introduces a story about when and how she first recognized that her prenatal exposure to the drug DES entailed significant consequences. The risks and problems of DES exposure had not been of focal concern to the respondent until she miscarried during the second trimester of her first pregnancy. Her story is about this experience and how it made the DES issue more central to her thinking and her life.

The respondent/narrator (N) begins her story with an utterance that would be defined as an Abstract in the Labov-Waletzky model of narrative analysis: "N: so (1) in any case, um (1.8) I then had some problems around, pregnancy, that sort of brought the whole issue of DES (1.5) t'much more t'the fore-front of my mind and [L: mhm] has made me much more, actively concerned about it, um I'll try and get my dates right" (Bell, 1983; numbers in parentheses refer to lengths of pauses in tenths of seconds; L is the interviewer/listener). Four epi-sodes follow, linked together temporally or causally each with its own Orientation and with narrative clauses that move the story forward. The story ends with her acceptance of the fact that her miscarriage was a result of her prenatal exposure to DES. In the first episode she reports a planned pregnancy that went smoothly at first: "yes I was planning to get pregnant and I got pregnant the first month that I, tried [L: mm] to get pregnant and that, you know went perfectly smoothly and had a wonderful p'pregnancy." But the pregnancy terminated in a miscarriage after five-and-a-half months. The second episode, immediately after and consequent to the miscarriage, occurred when a med-ical resident tells the respondent that the miscarriage might have resulted from her exposure to DES, but she "didn't believe her," thinking "she was sort of going though a whole list of things that she thought it might be and that was [L: mhm] sort of one out of, [L: mm,] whatever um and no." In the third episode, the woman's mother said, "Maybe this is due to the DES," but the respondent dismisses this as "ridiculous" because she couldn't "tolerate" having her mother "think that she had something to do with losing the baby." In the fourth and ter-minating episode of this story, the respondent accepts "the fact" that her miscarriage was "probably" due to DES exposure, be-cause the resident "had really done a lot of research" and pre-sented her with "a whole, scheme of how this could have happened," and "it made a lot more sense to me."

Bell tries to bring together the story-grammar approach and the Labov-Waletzky model, indicating how they provide differ-ent but closely related descriptions of narrative structure. In analyzing the stories and episodes in her interviews, she attends to how they are connected by temporal or causal conjunctions or phrases and how narrator/respondents use evaluative state-ments and conversational devices to suspend the story's action, build drama, and communicate the meaning of events. Bell observes that her respondent's account follows the temporal order of the real events. This matching of temporal ordering corresponds to the Labov-Waletzky criterion for a narrative, and she relies on this correspondence to define the account as a story and to specify its narrative structure.

Bell's analysis addresses both structure and content, that is, the textual and ideational functions. For example, she views the structure of the sequence of stories as representative of changes over the course of her respondent's life in accepting and adapting to the implications of her exposure to DES. She moves towards a more comprehensive model by including the interpersonal function, drawing upon Paget's work discussed earlier, and indicates how the interviewer/listener enters actively into the respondent/narrator's production of a story by the form and intent of her questions as well as by her assessments, acknowledgments, and silences. By distinguishing between the two roles that each participant may take, Bell is able to emphasize the features of this special context in which the story is told, namely, an interview. She suggests, from differences among questions and responses, that both parties are aware of their respective dual roles and that they attend to them in specific ways and manage shifts and transitions between them. For example, the respondent gives an "answer" to the interviewer's question and then shifts back to the "story" that as a narrator she is telling to a listener.

The complex ways in which the story develops through the movement into and out of these reciprocal dual roles is suggested by Bell's observations on the utterance with which the respondent begins her story of what "brought the whole issue of DES (1.5) t'much more t'the forefront of my mind." She says, "um I'll try and get my dates right." Bell notes that through this comment about dates the respondent "steps outside of her story," and that by remaining silent at that point she, the interviewer/listener, allows "her to return to the flow of her story. She shifts out of and back into her story, controlling this transition. By doing this, she acknowledges my dual role, as well as hers: I am an interviewer as well as listener-to-a-story. She is a subject in my investigation as well as a narrator" (p. 14).

A similar example comes at a later point, in the second episode, when Bell interrupts to ask after the report that the resident had implicated DES as a possible cause of the miscarriage, "did you say something to her when she said 'I think it's DES'? " Although the question content relates directly to the ongoing narrative, its form marks a shift out of its structure, and Bell views it as an interruption of the story. The respondent's reply is hesitant as she tries both to provide an adequate answer to the question as well as repair the interruption so that she can return to the story.

In an extended analysis of the story presented in Transcript 4, I provide an example of how the different approaches to narrative analysis may be brought together (Mishler, 1986). Drawing upon Labov's work for a structural analysis, I first reduced the full account shown in the transcript to a "core narrative" consisting of about 25 percent of the original text and then specified its constituents: Abstract, Orientation, Complicating Action, and Resolution. The key criterion for including a statement in the core narrative was that it be a narrative clause; thus the Complicating Action section consists of a sequence of temporally ordered clauses. Next, using evaluative comments to arrive at an intepretation of the "point" of the story, I undertook a second-stage reduction to determine if there was a more abstract structure of "Moves" that would help me understand the core narrative. This is, of course, Labov's 1982 strategy, in which he finds a triadic structure of a request–request denial–violent response as the basic plot in narratives of unexpected violent action. My analysis reveals a parallel but different triadic structure as the basic plot of this story: offer–refusal of offer–counter offer. The physician makes the first move by asking if it would "help" the respondent if he "reduced" his bill (065–066). The second move is the respondent's refusal to this offer: "And I said *no*. I wouldn't consider it, his reducing this bill at all" (077–078). The third move is the respondent's counter offer: "I said I was about to call you up . . . And I said, believe it or not, you're next up at bat . . . 'n I said Bill, if you can just hang in there I'll get your—I'll mail a check in about three or four days and that will start a run on this thing and we'll stamp the life out of it" (078–084). The story concludes with the Resolution that essentially restates the point first made at the beginning in the Abstract, that "we always *did* what we had to do some*how* we did it. We got through it" (013–015), but the Resolution is more succinct, "And that's what we did" (084–085). This relation between Abstract and Resolution gives us a sense of coherence and closure and supports the notion that what lies between these beginning and ending points is a connected narrative.

The abstract structure of Moves does not tell us what the content of the story means, nor why it was told in this particular context. A thematic analysis, based in part on the Agar-Hobbs model, of the various episodes in the story and the ways they are connected suggested that the story expresses general cultural values and at the same time represents the respondent's claim for a particular personal identity. By reporting repeated trials that he overcomes through his own efforts, the narrator represents himself as a self-reliant man who meets his responsibilities regardless of the cost to his personal desires.

The interview situation was traditional, and it had the usual asymmetric, hierarchical relationship between interviewee and interviewer. The respondent struggled against this definition of our relationship in many ways. His extended account may be understood as part of that struggle; he did not "answer" the original question and by continuing to talk he wrested control of the interview away from the interviewer. His repeated emphasis on his self-reliance, responsibility, and status must be placed in the context of this struggle for power within this type of interview. There is, in addition, a larger context to the interview. It was part of a study of his marriage and family history and, as he knew, his wife was also being interviewed. From his wife's interview we learned that he had had serious problems with alcoholism. These problems and their impact on his marriage and family were never mentioned in his interview with me. The respondent's identity claim as a responsible man must be understood as an effort to avoid this revelation, to protect himself, and to maintain his status vis-à-vis me.

This analysis, which addresses the textual, ideational, and interpersonal functions of narratives along with Paget's and Bell's studies, affirms the significance of the research interview as a special context for the structure and content of interview narratives. The interviewer's presence as a coparticipant is an unavoidable and essential component of the discourse, and an interviewer's mode of questioning influences a story's production. Differences in whether and how an interviewer encourages, acknowledges, facilitates, or interrupts a respondent's flow of talk have marked effects on the story that appears. Finally, interviewers and interviewees are both aware of and responsive to both the cultural and research contexts within which a particular interview is located.

Some Observations on Interview Research as Narrative Analysis

My primary aim in this chapter has been to demonstrate the feasibility and as well the exciting possibilities of an alternative to the mainstream tradition of interview research. Previous chapters prepared the way for this exploration of narrative-analytic methods, which I have suggested are particularly appropriate to studies of interviews as forms of discourse, that is, as speech events whose structure and meaning is jointly produced by interviewers and interviewees. The central and unifying idea of this proposal is that respondents' accounts can be understood as narratives, or stories. The highly selective survey of different models and methods for narrative analysis was designed to show that systematic research can be conducted within this perspective. In part this review may serve as a preliminary response to those investigators who, though aware of the limitations of the traditional approach, are hesitant to pursue an alternative until it can be shown that new methods are available to replace old ones.

The first task was to show that "answers" to questions often display the features of narratives. Instances reported here are of course only illustrative, but I do not think there are reasonable grounds to doubt their occurrence in many different types of interviews. Clearly, they may be elicited by direct questions to "tell a story," but they also appear as responses to narrow questions about specific topics and in individuals' reports in in-depth interviews of significant life experiences and events. When interviewers allow respondents to speak and when investigators are alert to the possibility and look for narratives, their ubiquity is evident.

That stories appear so often supports the view of some theorists that narratives are one of the natural cognitive and linguistic forms through which individuals attempt to order, organize, and express meaning. An argument to the contrary, namely, that narratives are unusual responses to special or idiosyncratic modes of interviewing, can neither be theoretically justified nor empirically supported. Rather, a stronger case can be made that the apparent absence of narratives in reports of interview studies is an artifact of standard procedures for conducting, describing, and analyzing interviews: interviewers interrupt respondents' answers and thereby suppress expression of their stories; when they appear, stories go unrecorded because they are viewed as irrelevant to the specific aims of specific questions; and stories that make it through these barriers are discarded at stages of coding and analysis.

Halliday's triad of linguistic functions—textual, ideational, and interpersonal—provided a useful framework for describing and contrasting different narrative-analytic approaches. Through this comparison I hoped to direct attention to implications of the third component of the proposed redefinition of interviewing, namely, that interpretation depends on a theory of discourse and meaning. For example, Labov's recent work is shaped by a key presupposition that narrative accounts represent the "functional" meanings of socially organized and normatively regulated interpersonal actions and relationships. For Agar and Hobbs, narratives express general cultural themes and values. Van Dijk focuses on cognitive processing; narratives are only one of many linguistic forms through which beliefs, underlying propositions about the world, and communicative intentions are expressed. In Paget's work narratives convey the ways that individuals attempt to arrive at a meaningful understanding of significant events in their lives.

These differences in focus and emphasis reflect in part the diverse interests and disciplines of investigators—as sociolinguists, anthropologists, cognitive psychologists, sociologists. I do not wish to put further weight in this context on these differences and their implications. Rather I note the diversity so as to highlight the fact that a variety of interests and theoretical concerns can be pursued through narrative analysis.[12]

Before closing this expository review I wish to comment briefly on two general questions, answers to which strongly influence the general lines and specific features of interview narrative studies. The first is whether an interview in its entirety is viewed as *the* story or if instead it is seen as containing "stories" along with other types of accounts. The aims, general shape, and specific features of a study are largely determined by how this question is answered. For example, contrasting answers are given by the Labov-Waletzky and Agar-Hobbs models. For the former a narrative is only one way of "recapitulating past experience." Within this conception a central research task is to establish criteria to distinguish narrative and nonnarrative stretches of an interview. As we have seen, much detailed analytic work is directed to this problem. Within the Agar-Hobbs conception, the research task is quite different. Because everything that a respondent says is revelant to and has a place in the story, effort is directed to determining how parts of the story fit together. Agar and Hobbs do this by specifying three types and levels of coherence; Bell approaches the problem by demarcating the boundaries of stories and examining how episodes and stories are then linked together.

The second question refers to the conceptualization, definition, and analytic use of the term *function*. The word has been used pervasively in this discussion, but it is evident that it has a variety of interpretations. Among the definitions listed in the *Oxford English Dictonary*, the one that seems closest to its generally intended meaning for narrative analysts is "the special kind of activity proper to anything; the mode of action by which it fulfills its purpose." Theorists vary in how they specify each of the components of this definition: in the units, or structures, of language that are their "things," in the "proper purposes" assigned to them, and in the designated "modes of action." For example, I have used Halliday's three linguistic functions to organize this review. These refer to inherent requirements of language, that is, linguistic elements must be organized into a structure, and texts and speech must be referential and must express a type of relationship between speaker/writer and hearer/reader. Because of its comprehensiveness, Halliday's framework permitted comparison of different approaches in terms of their relative emphasis on one or another function. A different interpretation is apparent in Propp's and Landau's analyses, respectively, of folktales and evolutionary theories. For these theorists functions refer to the narrative "work" of actions and events within the overall contexts of the story. And, to take a last example, Labov views narrative clauses as expressions of social and interpersonal functions, in this case how requests and responses to requests represent status relationships between speakers.

Differences among "functional" analyses are not resolved here. I do not anticipate a movement toward a universally accepted definition, and I am not convinced that such a movement would be particularly useful. Rather, my intention is to bring this issue to the attention of investigators so that they will be more explicit about their own definition and use of functional terms and categories. This would be a step in the direction of theoretical clarification because how functions are defined reflects assumptions about relations between language and meaning.

One last question warrants consideration. How can we assess the validity of a narrative interpretation? Katz (1983) observes that readers of qualitative field studies "repeatedly raise four questions about evidence. These may be characterized as four 'R's' that haunt participant observers in sociology" (p. 127). These "evidentiary questions" concern Representativeness, Reactivity, Reliability, and Replicability. They refer, respectively, to the well-known problems of the extent to which findings may be generalized; effects of observers on the data; criteria for selecting subsets of data for analysis and interpretation; and the possibility of repeating the study. In Katz's view, field researchers are too defensive in responding to these questions; they tend to accept the formal model of research, with its emphasis on experimental control and quantification, and try to fit their answers to that frame. Katz proposes to "undermine" the "habitual critical perspective" by developing "a rhetoric with which to respond more directly to standard methodological questions than claims of "discovery rather than verification' and 'pretesting' allow. The need is to outline an alternative perspective for interpreting such issues as representativeness, reactivity, reliability, and replicability, and simultaneously to indicate that the customary readings are at best arbitrary" (p. 130).

My experience echoes Katz's observations. Readers of earlier versions of this book have raised exactly these and other closely related questions, and my response also parallels Katz's argument. Although the underlying issues are fundamental ones for all modes of research, the specific form in which these questions are raised and the implicit criteria for assessing the adequacy of answers incorporate a particular model of research that field researchers, as well as other investigators engaged in various types of nonexperimental and nonquantitative types of studies, are attempting to replace. The development of an alternative model requires not only new methods of investigation and data analysis—such as those described here for narrative accounts and in the following chapter on interviewing practices—but a reformulation of these questions so that answers will bear more directly and more relevantly on these alternative modes of research. In Katz's terms, we need a new rhetoric.

How might we reconsider these issues? A good place to begin is with three presuppositions that appear to underlie these questions, particularly when they are addressed to investigators using nontraditional approaches: (1) the questions imply that the issues of reliability, validity, and replicability have been effectively resolved in the kind of studies modeled on the experimental paradigm that rely on statistical analyses of quantitative measures; (2) the questions presume that these issues have been ignored by those engaged in nontraditional forms of research, implying that they have been too easily satisfied with imprecise methods, unrepeatable analyses, and vague and ungrounded inferences; (3) the questions assume that there is one "true" interpretation of an array of data and further that this interpretation may be determined by standard, universally applicable technical procedures. None of these presuppositions is well founded.

The history of debate within psychology about the concept of validity is a particularly revealing indicator of unresolved problems within the mainstream tradition. In comparison to an earlier period, twenty to thirty years ago, there is now more open controversy and more receptivity to nontraditional approaches. This change reflects increasingly widespread recognition of the inadequacies of narrowly defined methodological solutions and of the intimate and inherent entanglement of validation with theoretical and substantive considerations. Levy (1981) in his presidential address to the British Psychological Association makes the general point that "we have a long tradition of labelling certain difficulties as 'methodological problems' as though 'method' in our subject is separable from what might be called 'substance'. Methodological problems are disguised substantive problems" (p. 265). He observes that we often "speak of 'validating' rather than 'discovering the meaning of'. And we are tempted to speak of such things as objectivity, truth, proof, and methodology where I believe we mean to refer to the more human and social qualities of communicability, generalizability, plausibility, and interpretability" (p. 269).

In a paper that has had a marked and continuing influence on discussion of the validation problem, Cronbach and Meehl (1955) distinguish four types of validity: predictive, concurrent, content, and construct. They emphasize the importance of theory in the validation process and the special significance of construct validation, which is involved "whenever a test is to be interpreted as a measure of some attribute or quality which is not 'operationally defined.' " This process is not to be identified with particular methods "but by the orientation of the investigator" (p. 282).

A reformulation advanced by Campbell and Stanley (1963) was in the ascendancy for many years. Their distinction was between "internal" and "external" validity, the former referring to the specific findings of a particular study and the latter to the generalizability of findings to other populations and situations. In apparent contrast to Cronbach and Meehl, Campbell and Stanley gave first priority to internal validity, "the basic minimum without which any experiment is uninterpretable: Did in fact the experimental treatments make a difference in this specific experimental instance" (p. 5). In their comparative analysis of different experimental and quasi-experimental designs, they developed the strategy, which became part of every investigator's methodological equipment, of assessing the "threats to validity" that were either controlled for or left uncontrolled in each design.

Differences in viewpoint persist, but the major proponents now see themselves in essential agreement but with slightly different emphases reflecting their specific research commitments. The result is both a deeper understanding of the problem and a more flexible approach than is assumed in the questions about Katz's four R's with which we began. Cronbach (1980, p. 7) remains convinced that external validity is of primary importance. In his sixtieth "thesis" for evaluation research, he states: "External validity—that is, the validity of inferences that go beyond the data—is the crux; increasing internal validity by elegant design often reduces relevance." Still more recently, Cronbach (1982) reviews the history of close exchanges with Campbell on these issues and remarks on the latter's response to a draft of his summary volume on the design of evaluation research: "Campbell insisted to my surprise that he was in nearly complete agreement with me" (p. xv). In a section entitled "The Emerging Reconciliation" (pp. 26–30), he enlarges on the areas of agreement and differences in emphasis.

How Campbell's views have altered is evident in recent work. Although internal validity remains fundamental, the typology of validity types each with its own "threats" has been expanded to a set of four: statistical conclusion, internal, construct, and external (Cook and Campbell, 1979). In this extended revision of his earlier work with Stanley (Campbell and Stanley, 1963), there is early stress on the concepts of validity and invalidity as referring to "the best available approximation to the truth or

falsity of propositions, including propositions about cause . . .
we should always use the modifier "approximately" when referring to validity, since one can never know what is true. At best,
one can know what has not yet been ruled out as false" (Cook
and Campbell, 1979, p. 37).

In the present context Campbell's (1979) revised view of the
value of case studies is worth noting. Rejecting his own earlier
"caricature of the single case study approach" (p. 54) and observing that case studies need not be guilty of all the faults he
attributed to them, Campbell comments that he had "overlooked
a major source of discipline" (p. 57), namely, that investigators
generate many interdependent predictions from their theories
and do not retain a theory unless most predictions are confirmed. "In some sense, [the investigator] has tested the theory
with degrees of freedom coming from the multiple implications
of any one theory. The process is a kind of pattern-matching in
which there are many aspects of the pattern demanded by theory that are available for matching with his observations on the
local setting" (p. 57). In the course of reaching his conclusion
that "qualitative common-sense knowing is not replaced by
quantitative knowing. Rather, quantitative knowing has to trust
and build upon the qualitative, including ordinary perception"
(p. 66), Campbell assigns special significance to the "narrative
history" section of quantitative evaluation studies: "evaluation
studies are uninterpretable without this, and most would be
better interpreted with more . . . The narrative history is an
indispensable part of the final report, and the best qualitative
methods should be used in preparing it" (p. 52).

This brief excursion into the history of debate about the concept of validity is intended primarily to document the failure,
recognized by many researchers within the mainstream tradition, of simple, technical solutions that are often presumed when
"qualitative" researchers are asked to justify their interpretations. It has become clear that the critical issue is not the determination of one singular and absolute "truth" but the assessment
of the relative plausibility of an interpretation when compared
with other specific and potentially plausible alternative interpretations. Awareness of the range of "threats" to the internal va-

lidity of a study is an important aspect of such an assessment, but other features of a study are of equal importance and require equal consideration. These include the care with which the research process, for example, observing and interviewing, is carried out and documented; the specification of rules that guide analysis; the explication of a theoretical framework and of the ways that inferences and interpretations of analyses are grounded in and related to it; the judgments of various interested audiences, including the subjects of a study, as to the plausibility and meaningfulness of interpretations. With regard to the latter, Cronbach (1980, p. 11) transforms the notion of plausibility into a social judgment of "credibility." His ninety-fifth and last thesis for researchers is, "Scientific quality is not the principal standard; an evaluation should aim to be comprehensible, correct, and complete, and credible to partisans on all sides."

For their part, researchers from many disciplines who engage in nonexperimental, nonquantitative forms of research would find these current views and approaches of more traditional researchers quite compatible with their own. For example, the emphasis on threats to validity that is central to the Campbell-Stanley and Cook-Campbell analyses closely resembles Tagg's (1985) discussion of problems in assessing the reliability of life stories. Referring to Cronbach and associates' (1972) "generalizability theory," Tagg argues that a statistical measure of reliability is "only one measure of resilience against sources of error" and that "researchers should not be concerned about the reliability of life story methods in the abstract but rather should ask what the plausible rival explanations are, for example, forgetting or retrospective reconstruction, and what defenses are possible against such interpretive competition? (p. 188). As aids to this endeavor Tagg provides a detailed "facet analysis" of the stages in life-story interviewing research (p. 165) and outlines the main sources of error (p. 191) as well as ways in which they may be controlled.[13]

In the context of this discussion, we may now return to the specific problem of evaluating the validity of interpretations of interview narratives. How, for example, might we assess the "plausibility" of Labov's (1982) interpretation of narratives of unexpected violence. Recall that he transforms each of three accounts, elicited by direct questions in interviews, into "core narratives" and then, to explain the temporal ordering of events, proposes an abstract set of three sequential "Moves": a request, a denial of the request that denies the legitimacy of and thereby poses a threat to the requester's social status, a violent act. What "sources of error" or "threats to validity" remain uncontrolled, reducing the "resilience" of this interpretation and at the same time supporting "rival" interpretations?

Katz's (1983) typology of the four R's is a useful though preliminary framework for examining these questions. How "representative" are these accounts? For purposes of illustration, two different threats to their "external validity" may be noted, factors that may limit our confidence in their generalizability. First, the stories all refer to acts of violence by men against men. Would this interpretation apply to women? Are issues of "social status" less salient for women, implying that threats to women's status relationships may be less likely to provoke violence? Are other issues more salient, such that, for example, threats to the stability of relationships may result in violent responses? Second, Labov assumes that the interpretation of narrative accounts applies to actual episodes of unexpected violence, but there are no detailed observations of such episodes (nor independent reports of those related in the stories themselves). Labov does not examine, either conceptually or empirically, the various degrees and forms of relation between narrative accounts and actual events. Generalizations to the latter based on interpretations of the former have little warrant and are therefore not plausible.

The relative lack of attention to the interview situation and to the role of the interviewer in Labov's study, a point noted in my earlier discussion, leaves open the question of how these accounts may have been affected by various features of the research context. This is the problem of reactivity. In both structure and content these retrospective reconstructions of long-past events may reflect how respondents perceive and attempt to deal with differences between their own and the interviewer's "worlds" (an issue explored by Agar and Hobbs, 1982, in their analysis of addict life histories), or the ways the account is a joint production of the discourse between interviewee and interviewer (Bell, 1983), or the implicit claim for a valued social identity that is embedded in the story (Mishler, 1986). Each of these unexamined possibilities remains a threat to the plausibility of Labov's interpretive model, to its comprehensiveness and adequacy for the particular accounts, and to its generalizability.

Similar questions may be raised about reliability—What criteria entered into the selection of these three accounts from the corpus of interviews? Were there negative instances and how did they influence development of the interpretation?—and, in light of these various considerations, about the replicability of the study. The general point is not to criticize Labov's work but to show how a critical assessment of interpretations of life stories and interview narratives may be developed by focusing on problems that are central to this mode of research rather than on abstract, standardized, technical, and often inappropriate criteria and methods drawn from a quite different research tradition. Systematic examination of "threats to plausibility" in any one study provides guidelines for other investigators and helps to clarify significant theoretical and empirical issues for further study. The aim of this exercise, like Campbell's (1979) analysis of the merits and difficulties of case studies, is to "offer a few suggestions for improving the discipline such studies offer as probes for theory" (p. 60).

In my list of the presuppositions of questions commonly addressed to qualitative researchers, I referred to the assumption of one "true" interpretation. Much of what has been said here suggests the continued viability of alternative interpretations that are sifted, compared, and evaluated for plausibility through the extended and diverse histories of research on particular topics. Beyond this array, however, there remain alternative theoretical perspectives that generate different questions and do not compete directly with one another as "rival" explanations. A psychoanalytically oriented researcher would have a different series of questions to ask about personal narratives of unexpected violence and would interpret these accounts in a way markedly different from Labov's sociological model. And an oral historian interested in changes over time in relations between the social and political order and forms of deviance is likely to ask questions other than those we find in Agar and Hobbs's analysis of addict life histories. Research generated within and guided by each perspective may still be assessed for its plausibility in terms of the framework suggested here.

Brenner (1981, p. vii) develops a view of method in the social sciences with which I am in full accord, and his general observations serve well to bring this chapter to a close. He proposes to develop a line of "methodological reasoning" that would be "useful in reconstructing the established measurement paradigm in the social sciences which maintains that social and psychological processes in data collection are either unproblematic or appear as sources of error and data contamination to be eliminated or controlled." Against this paradigm he argues for a "realistic" approach where "data collection practices should be based on knowledge of the social and psychological processes that enable, and constrain, the use of methods instead of purely normative expectations concerning measurement adequacy." Within such a perspective, methodologists would be encouraged to develop a social and psychological theory of measurement that attended to actual practices, to develop new methods that "would enable more intimate familiarity with social life, and, therefore, more valid measurement," and to "become careful and cautious in their use of methods, knowing that unbiased measurement in socially reactive data collection settings is unlikely, if not usually impossible." The aim of such a program is to provide "a convincing exposition of a methodology which we wish to practice as particular forms of social life."

Meaning in Context and the Empowerment of Respondents

A dominant theme of this book is that meanings are contextually grounded. This proposition is central to both my critique of current practice and my recommendations for an alternative approach. Adopting this perspective and following through its implications requires a radical transformation of the traditional approach to interviewing. Earlier chapters addressed several contextual issues, for example, effects on responses of question form and order, the neglect in mainstream research of cultural frameworks of meaning in eliciting and interpreting responses, and the joint construction by interviewers and respondents of particular contexts of relevance through which they achieve a shared understanding of their discourse. These specific points will not be repeated here. Rather, in focusing on this theme for separate discussion I hope to situate issues of research practice within a larger sociocultural and sociopolitical context and therefore provide a point of departure for enlarging our consideration of interviewing as a method.

In the mainstream tradition the interviewee-interviewer relationship is marked by a striking asymmetry of power; this is the central structuring feature of interviews as research contexts. The alternatives to standard practice that will be discussed here are directed toward the empowerment of respondents. I will be concerned primarily with the impact of different forms of practice on respondents' modes of understanding themselves and the world, on the possibility of their acting in terms of their own interests, on social scientists' ways of working and theorizing, and on the social functions of scientific knowledge. It need hardly be said that these are large questions and that this effort is preliminary and exploratory, intended to open them up for further discussion rather than to answer them definitively.

The particular ways these questions are framed within the contextual perspective adopted here will become clear as the discussion proceeds. It may be useful, however, to foreshadow the main line of argument by stating briefly one of its critical themes. Namely, my intent is to shift attention away from investigators' "problems," such as technical issues of reliability and validity, to respondents' problems, specifically, their efforts to construct coherent and reasonable worlds of meaning and to make sense of their experiences. This shift leads to the general question of how different types of interviews facilitate or hinder respondents' efforts to make sense of what is happening to them and around them. Further, it brings into the foreground the hidden problem of power, both in the interview situation itself and in the mainstream tradition of social science research. Whose interests are served by the asymmetry of power between interviewer and respondent? Who benefits from investigators' control of the interpretation, dissemination, and use of "findings"? A central task in what follows is to find ways to empower respondents so that they have more control of the processes through which their words are given meaning.[1]

The effort to empower respondents and the study of their responses as narratives are closely linked. They are connected through the assumption, elaborated in the preceding chapter, that one of the significant ways through which individuals make sense of and give meaning to their experiences is to organize them in a narrative form. As we shall see, various attempts to restructure the interviewee-interviewer relationship so as to empower respondents are designed to encourage them to find and speak in their own "voices." It is not surprising that when the interview situation is opened up in this way, when the balance of power is shifted, respondents are likely to tell "stories." In sum, interviewing practices that empower respondents also produce narrative accounts. There is, however, an additional implication of empowerment. Through their narratives people may be moved beyond the text to the possibilities of action. That is, to be empowered is not only to speak in one's own voice and to tell one's own story, but to apply the understanding arrived at to action in accord with one's own interests.

The decontextualizing features of standard research interviews are one expression of a widespread sociocultural trend. The shift in focus and dirction of this discussion to the impact of research practices on respondents may be placed in this larger context by beginning with Trow's (1981) observations on contemporary American culture. In a critical essay, with the evocative title *Within the Context of No Context*, Trow describes the psychological impact of forms of presentations in the mass media that either exclude or obscure real and valid contexts of events and experiences. The style of news reporting on television, for example, the serial presentation of brief reports of unrelated events, strips away particular historical and social contexts. By giving each piece of news relatively equal treatment—in the time allotted to them and through the standardized mien and delivery of reporters—differences among them in significance are removed.

The result, Trow argues, is destruction of the human scale of experience, which he refers to as the "middle distance." Confronted with the systematic erasure of appropriate and relevant contexts of understanding, individuals find it difficult to make sense of what is happening and consequently feel confused and estranged: "The middle distance fell away, so the grids (from small to large) that had supported the middle distance fell into disuse and ceased to be understandable. Two grids remained. The grid of two hundred million and the grid of intimacy. Everything else fell into disuse . . . The distance between these two grids was very great. The distance was very frightening . . . People began to lose a sense of what distance was and of what the usefulness of distance might be" (p. 7). Trow lists a variety of devices used in mass media that are intended to repair these problems, such as the introduction of "false" and "ad hoc" contexts and the use of stereotypes and other "abandoned shells" of meaning. These efforts fail because they do not address the source of the problem, that is, the distortion of meaning that results from context-stripping practices.

Trow's characterization of the world as it is presented through television, popular magazines, and other media bears a remarkable and disturbing similarity to the world presented to respondents through the specialized medium of the standard interview schedule: that "world" is abstract, fragmented, precategorized, standardized, divorced from personal and local contexts of relevance, and with its meanings defined and controlled by researchers. Trow's two remaining grids, "the grid of two hundred million and the grid of intimacy," are analogous to the two primary "grids" of social science research, namely, large-scale statistical analyses of population aggregates on the one hand and case studies on the other. The distance between these two research grids is very great and is not bridged by ad hoc hypotheses and speculative inferences about relations between the individual and society, whether they are advanced by social scientists or by society's citizens.

The parallels between the two scenarios suggest that traditional research practices may be alienating in their effects on respondents and therefore may further reinforce the deeper and more pervasive sources of alienation in contemporary society. That is, the standard interview through both its form and the hierarchic structure of the interviewee-interviewer relationship tends to obscure relations between events and experiences and to disrupt individuals' attempts to make coherent sense of what is happening to them and around them. In stating this problem forcefully I am countering the usual notion that research methods are "neutral," that is, merely technical instruments for recording and describing reality that do not in themselves change reality. Recognizing that all methods have consequences, that the form and content of interviews affect respondents, allows us to bring forward the question of how interviewing may be changed so as to be less alienating.

Investigators have not been totally unconcerned about effects on respondents of research procedures, but their concerns tend to focus on such issues as biasing effects of experimental interventions or questions, confidentiality, and risks to subjects of invasive procedures. With respect to bias, for example, a well-explored problem in cohort and panel studies is the influence of a first interview on responses in later interviews. In experimental studies differential effects of variations in preexperimental procedures on different groups in a research design has received detailed attention (Campbell and Stanley, 1963; Cook and Campbell, 1979). For those concerned with problems of confidentiality, a strong tradition, which has been institutionalized in recent years through Human Studies Committees and by formal regulations specifying the rights of subjects and governing research on human subjects, enjoins investigators to protect the privacy of respondents and to assure confidentiality. Informed-consent procedures are intended to minimize negative social and personal consequences and serve the purpose of allowing subjects to assess the risks of their participation in a study.

Issues of bias, confidentiality, and risk are important, but they differ from the question raised here, How are respondents' views and understandings of themselves and the world shaped by the form and context of research interviews? Trow's observations about the alienating impact of forms of representation that replace real contexts with artificial ones alert us as investigators to the possibility that respondents may be affected similarly by research interviews that strip away natural contexts of meaning from both questions and responses.

The text of an interview schedule is of course only one element of an interview situation that may produce estrangement and alienation in respondents. Problems of context and the meaning and impact of specific types of questions are related intimately to the relative power of interviewees and interviewers. The marked asymmetry of power manifest in current forms of research practice reflects more than the essential feature of an interview as a speech event, that is, a situation with defined roles for questioners and respondents. It is indicative beyond this feature, of an interviewer's relatively total control over the structuring of meaning.

In a standard interview respondents are presented with a predetermined scheme of relevances: topics, definitions of events, categories for response and evaluation are all introduced, framed, and specified by interviewers, who determine the adequacy and appropriateness of responses. Finally, researchers through their analyses and reports define the "meaning" of responses and findings, whereas respondents have no opportunity to comment upon interpretations of their words and intentions. This way of doing research takes away from respondents their right to "name" their world (Freire, 1970). Stated somewhat extremely and from the perspective of respondents, interview research by excluding the biographical rooting and contextual grounding of respondents' personal and social webs of meaning bears a resemblance to a "degradation ceremony" (Garfinkel, 1956) or an identity-stripping process (Goffman, 1961).

The intent of this relatively harsh rhetoric about potential negative impacts on respondents of standard interviewing practices is to confront all of us as investigators with implications of our work that are rarely considered. If we move beyond a view of contextual problems as "merely" technical to recognition of their sociocultural and political significance, we may be able to open up possibilities for alternative forms of interviewing. How can we redress the asymmetry of power inherent to the traditional approach to interviewing and restore control to respondents over what they mean by what they say?

Alternative Roles for Interviewers and Interviewees: The Redistribution of Power

Movement in the direction of reducing the asymmetry of power in interview research is demonstrated by the work of investigators who have altered the standard role definitions of interviewee and interviewer as respondent and researcher. A review of these efforts suggests potentially different types and degrees of change in relative power. These types of role redefinitions may be characterized briefly by the following terms referring respectively to the relationship between interviewee and interviewer as informant and reporter, as research collaborators, and as learner/actor and advocate. Taking on the roles of each successive pair in this series involves a more comprehensive and more radical transformation of the power relationship inherent in traditional roles, and each succeeding pair of roles relies on and absorbs the earlier ones. Further, each successively expands the contribution of interviewees' understandings and interests as contexts for interpretation.

Informants and Reporters

A view of interviewees as informants or as competent observers and interviewers as reporters is often found in ethnographic research. Trying to characterize cultures as patterns of meaning, anthropologists rely on what the members of a culture can tell them. As investigators they see their task as reporting members' understandings, that is, their cultural realities, as accurately as possible.[2] In research in other social and behavioral sciences the balance tips more toward the explication or development of the views and theories of investigators. In this type of study interviewees are defined as research subjects and are pressed into the service of providing data relevant to, and sometimes testing the adequacy of, investigators' theories rather than being asked to inform us about their theories.

The complex interdependence of various components of a study as they reflect the roles prescribed for interviewees and interviewers may be illustrated with reference to the problem of confidentiality. I noted earlier that confidentiality is viewed as a "right" of respondents. The assurance we give interviewees that they will not be identified by name and that our reports will include only aggregate data and statistical analyses are intended to "protect" their privacy. There is also a common assumption among researchers that this guarantee of anonymity is more likely to produce "truthful" and candid responses.

A contrasting view may be found in the work of anthropologists with a different conception of their own and their respondents' roles, who often specify the names of their key informants. To cite just one example, Hymes (1981, p. 89) not only identifies the individual who is the source of a primary text in his analysis of Chinookan narratives, but specifies the context and date of its production: "a booth in the Rainbow Cafe," "at night after work," "on the night of 25 July 1956." Hymes's specification of these particulars reflects his theoretical interest in narratives as "performances." In addition it is consistent with the social and political values that inform his work, namely, respect for the culture of his informants and the aim of reporting and thereby helping to preserve their distinctive patterns of cultural meaning. Within this perspective identification is a way through which members of the culture retain control over, that is, continue to "own," their ways of "naming the world."

In research settings where emphasis is placed on confidentiality, such an approach may appear strange and a violation of the right to privacy. For example, in the study on creativity referred to earlier Paget (1983a) wished to give the artists she was interviewing the option of being identified. She was asking them to talk about their own works and their personal experiences as artists and planned to use verbatim interview excerpts in her reports. Like Hymes, she viewed her respondents as informants with the "right" to have their views represented as belonging to them, if they so wished. Her artist-informants had no difficulty with this proposal, but the Human Studies Committee did. The committee's rules and experiences reflected a deep concern with problems of confidentiality. Its members were familiar with informed-consent procedures that provide assurances of confidentiality and were sensitive to different degrees of certainty that could be attached to such assurances. But the "right" to be identified was strange to them.

These examples are not intended as an argument for the general identification of respondents. Nor am I proposing that a concern with protecting respondents through assurances of confidentiality is either misplaced or illegitimate. There are many situations where respondents wish to control the conditions under which their opinions will be made public; they want to be responsible for choosing where and when and to whom they will say what they think and feel. These situations include, for example, subordinates' attitudes about their superiors in a work setting, neighbors' attitudes about how other parents raise their children, minority political or social views in a community. In these instances confidentiality is consistent with the aim of empowering respondents in the sense that they retain control over the circumstances under which their personal views enter into the discourse with others in their social worlds.

In other situations the assurance of confidentiality does not appear to be in the interests of informants because it parallels and reinforces the decontextualizing effects of the standard interview and the asymmetry of power between interviewee and interviewer. Through the routine assurance of confidentiality interviewees are told that they will be treated as part of an anonymous mass; not only do the questions refer to anyone and not to them in particular, but their answers will not be connected to them. They will not be held personally responsible for what they say, nor will they be credited as individuals for what they say and think. In brief, they are deprived of their own voices. Katz's (1983) observations about relationships between researchers and subjects in field research are relevant here. One of the strengths of field studies, Katz argues, is that researchers and subjects come to recognize and treat each other as "significant others." Subjects respond to the researcher not simply as an "objective" scientist but as a person with personal qualities and views, and their behavior toward the investigator resembles their behavior with others in their own worlds. Researchers, on their part, have to be attentive to the fit between their interpretations and their subjects' understanding, which serves as a validity check on their findings.

These comments on the issue of confidentiality are intended to suggest the complexity and the range of implications for research practice, including preconditions for research such as informed-consent procedures, of the rather modest shift from interviewee-interviewer roles to informant-reporter roles. Taken-for-granted assumptions about the aims and ethics of routine procedures as well as about the responsibilities of investigators to their subjects are made problematic and opened up for review and relection. Redefining respondents as informants, explicitly introducing personal contexts as grounds for interpretation, granting respondents the right to control how meanings are constructed from their responses as well as control over whether and how they will be identified—all confront us as investigators with questions that must be thought through in fresh ways at each stage of the research process in each particular study.

Research Collaborators

A further step in the direction of reducing the power differential in an interview is to accept interviewees as collaborators, that is, as full participants in the development of the study and in the analysis and interpretation of data. Laslett and Rapoport (1975, p. 969), for example, refer to their approach to a study involving several interviews with each member of a family as "collaborative interviewing and interactive research." Working within a clinical, psychoanalytically informed perspective, they are particularly concerned with how unexpressed transference and countertransference feelings of interviewees and interviewers may affect both the interview itself and interpretation. They recommend various training and supervisory procedures to help interviewers be aware of these issues so as to improve the "internal validity" of the data.

Proposing that feedback be given to respondents, "consistent with the collaborative, reciprocating element in the research contract," Laslett and Rapoport urge researchers to tell "respondents something about how the data are viewed and will be used" (p. 974). They showed drafts of their reports to respondents so that they could correct errors of fact and then attempted to resolve disagreements of interpretation with them. Further, they note the importance of having "respondents' permission to publish," observing that disputed material may be omitted or presented as a "dissenting account" (p. 974). Osherson (1980) circulated the prepublication draft of his book on midlife career changes to the several men whose interviews were used as primary case studies. He reports their responses in

a postscript included in his book, particularly those to his interpretations of his interviews with them. Willis (1977, pp. 194–195)
includes as an appendix to his report of an ethnographic participant observation study of working-class adolescents an "edited transcription" of a group discussion with some of his subjects
"centered on how my role as a researcher had been seen and
what the 'results' of the research meant to them."

These few examples represent efforts to give respondents'
own views a place in a research report. Nonetheless the nature
of collaboration in these studies is quite limited. Respondents'
views may be presented, usually as a postscript, but the research
aims and methods, as well as lines of analysis and interpretation,
remain very much under the control of the investigator. In this
sense the focus remains on researchers' problems. Laslett and
Rapoport wish to ensure the "validity" of their data and avoid
errors of fact and judgment. For them and for Osherson, respondents provide a check on their interpretations and are given
an opportunity to have their views heard, although because
decisions about what, how, and where to publish are still the
investigator's, the opportunity is a somewhat restricted one.

A collaborative relationship is more closely approximated in
an interuniversity project on women's development described
by Belenky, Clinchy, Goldberger, and Tarule (1981–82). The
relatively unstructured interviews include a series of open-ended
questions, and respondents are asked to tell their life stories in
their own "voices." Copies of interview transcripts are returned
and reviewed together by investigators and interviewees. The
work of understanding the materials is a joint effort and understandings arrived at enter into planning and development of
next stages of the study. In addition, research findings are used
as the basis for a variety of other activities, such as workshops,
seminars, and courses, directed to helping women with family,
career, and developmental issues that emerge in the interviews.
The investigators also note certain positive effects on their respondents' lives of having participated in the study, such as a
"self-reported sense of change following the initial interview . . .
For some, the interview was the first step toward 'gaining a
voice' " (Belenky et al., 1981–82, p. 7).

An example of collaborative research involving ethnographic methods rather than interviewing is reported by Florio and Walsh (1981). In this study of classroom behavior, collaboration was not planned in advance. Both the researcher and teacher began with rather traditional views of their roles and the aims of the study and with some uncertainty and wariness of each other. Neither anticipated that they would shape the research together as the work proceeded and that their roles would come to blend so that the study became the "joint enterprise of the 'participant observer' and the 'observant participant'" (p. 91). Regarding the value of the approach, Florio and Walsh conclude that "this way of working treats the teacher and children not as objects of study, but as active subjects of great interest and importance. The teacher's opinions are valued. She is seen as a vital member of the research team . . . her cooperation and insight are essential to the process of inquiry. The entire research operation becomes more congenial and the findings beneficial to all involved. Both parties go away having gained something of value" (pp. 99–100).

Another, more comprehensive type of collaboration is described by Thompson (1978) in his review and exposition of oral-history research. Arguing that the "cooperative nature of the oral history approach has led to a radical questioning of this one-sided process," namely, that the professional historian takes away information to interpret and present to other historians, Thompson asserts that "through oral history the community can, and should, be given the confidence to write its own history" (p. 14). He reports a number of such studies including, for example, a collective project of residents of Hackney in East London called the "People's Autobiography." Members of the group conduct interviews, collect other materials on the community and its residents, and publish accounts of people's lives. With the intent of giving "back to people their own history," the project aims "on the one hand, to build up through a series of individual accounts a composite history of life and work in Hackney, and, on the other, to give people confidence in their own memories and interpretations of the past, their ability to contribute to the writing of history—confidence, too, in their own words: in short, in themselves" (p. 15).

These last examples of collaborative research, particularly the People's Autobiography, approximate what I have distinguished as a third alternative to the traditional researcher-subject relationship, one in which the departure from the usual power distribution is most marked.

Learners/Actors and Advocates

On February 26, 1972, a dam collapsed and several communities in the Buffalo Creek valley in Appalachia, West Virginia, were destroyed in the resulting flood. Erikson (1976), hired by attorneys representing residents of these communities in their suit for damages against the local coal company, was to study, document, and assess the social and psychological impacts of this disaster. The individual and community "traumas" that he reported were used as supporting evidence in the legal claim for damages.

This study is a clear example of advocacy; his subjects were actors in a world of competing interests, and his work was intended to serve their interests. Although Erikson, as a research sociologist, was attentive to methodological and theoretical issues, the pace, methods, and aims of the study were determined primarily by the needs of his subjects as litigants rather than by general sociological interests and criteria. Erikson observes that "it is no easy matter to overcome the suspicion with which strangers are greeted there," (p. 13) but that the research task was eased remarkably and that people were open and forthcoming in his interviews because of his association with the law firm and his informants' understanding of the purpose of his research. Accepting the obligation to document and represent their views and experiences, he "relies heavily on words spoken by the survivors of the Buffalo Creek disaster," (p. 13), words that he tries to reproduce "in their original form" without "tidying up the grammar" (p. 15).

A radical reformulation of the interviewee-researcher roles into the roles of learner/actor and advocate was developed explicitly by Anita L. Mishler (1978–80) in her study of college students' experiences. The aim of the research was to collect information about students' lives that could be used to design residential environments and extracurricular programs that would be less alienating to the students and more conducive to the integration of academic work and their nonacademic lives. Mishler realized that standard interviews and questionnaires duplicated exactly those impersonal, abstract, and fragmented features of undergraduate life that she was trying to change. Rejecting that approach, she constructed an interview schedule that was intended to facilitate students' efforts to learn about their problems and to reflect on possible solutions through the interview itself.

For example, rather than asking standard attitude questions about university programs, Mishler asked the students to reflect upon how they connected their course work to other parts of their lives and to consider the problems and implications of trying to make such connections. In successive interviews she reported back both their own responses and the general trend among their classmates as background to their continuing discussion together and as information that would be helpful to students' efforts to understand and integrate different aspects of their lives. One result of this process was that students discovered that there were others who shared their experiences, which fostered both their sense of community and their efforts to work collectively in pursuit of common goals. Thus, the research helped to reduce the sense of alienation among students and to empower them. In these ways and in her own efforts to implement research findings through new programs, Mishler moved beyond the collaborative relationship to become an advocate of students' interests.

A closely related approach that radically restructures the researcher-subject relationship and encompasses much more than interviewing is described by Mies (1983) as part of a general effort to develop "a new methodological approach consistent with the political aims of the women's movement" (p. 118). Mies urges the replacement of traditional social science postulates, for example, that it is value free and neutral, with an emphasis on *"conscious partiality* . . . through partial identification with the research subjects" (p. 122) directed to serving "the interests of dominated, exploited and oppressed groups, particularly women" (p. 123). In her view research becomes part of the general political struggle "for women's emancipation" (p. 124).

Mies reports an action-study that linked documentation of the seriousness and extent of violence against wives to the establishment of a shelter for battered women. Using various political tactics, such as street demonstrations and media publicity on the problem as they documented it through interviews, the researchers sucessfully pressed a reluctant city administration to recognize the problem and eventually provide a subsidy for the shelter. At the same time they conducted life-history interviews with women who came to the shelter, reviewed these interviews in group discussions, and developed a play, which they then filmed, based on common elements and themes in the histories. Mies concludes that "the systematic documentation of their life histories has the effect that their own subjective biography assumes an objective character . . . serves a very practical purpose . . . in order to re-organize their lives . . . Apart from the individual, practical and theoretical dimensions, the writing-down and discussion of life histories also has political and action-oriented dimensions, aiming at creating a new collective consciousness among women and mobilizing them for further social action" (pp. 134–135).

This series of examples, marking degrees of change in the relative power of interviewees and interviewers and the associated transformation of the interview situation as a research context, brings us back full circle to Trow's observations about the alienating impact of false and/or abstract contexts. Erikson's study of the Buffalo Creek disaster, Anita Mishler's study of students' lives, and Mies's action-study with battered women, in addition to having other consequences, attempt to counter such negative effects.

It is evident even from brief characterizations of these studies that the different impacts on respondents of alternative approaches are paralleled by significant changes in the role of investigators as social scientists as well as in the nature of scientific knowledge and its uses. Yielding control to itnerviewees of the flow and content of the interview, entering into a collaborative relationship, attending to what and how interviewees may learn from their efforts to respond meaningfully to questions within the context of their own worlds of experience, giving them a voice in the interpretation and use of findings, serving as advocates of their interests—all these "research methods" radically alter the standard definition of a researcher's role and aims.

The Impact on Our Views of Scientific Knowledge

Bakan's (1967) provocative essay on the "mystery-mastery" complex in psychological research suggests a way to consider the potential impact on our views of scientific knowledge of changes in the relative power of interviewees and interviewers. Bakan asserts that there are two incompatible but jointly pursued objectives of traditional scientific research: "to keep the nature of the psyche a mystery and master human behavior" (pp. 37–38). He argues further that the traditional emphasis on discovery of general laws and on hypothesis testing are in the service of preserving both objectives, despite their incompatibility.

> The service of the mastery objective is patent. The mystery is preserved by formulating these laws on the basis of research in which the information concerning the presumptive regularities are concealed from the subjects, and by never allowing a theoretical place for the knowledge of the regularities as factors in human functioning. One of the most ubiquitous fears of investigators is that the human subjects will not be "naive," that they might be aware of the nature of the phenomenon under investigation . . . that human beings make use of generalizations concerning the nature of human functioning in their functioning . . . is one of the factors involved in the mystery of the psyche which is systematically excluded in the search for laws . . . The elevation of the hypothesis-testing stage to the point where it is conceived of as practically the entire investigatory enterprise is the service of the mystery-mastery complex. The preconception of the alternatives, and the disciplined limitation of the investigation to them, cuts out the possibility of surprise, the learning of something that was not

thought of beforehand . . The obligation to preconceive the alternatives tends to preserve the mystery of the psyche, by eliminating what is not "proper" . . . The mastery objective is served by selection of preconceived alternatives which fulfill it and elimination of others. (pp. 43–45)

Although Bakan focuses on the experimental method, his observations are similar to mine on interviewing. Given that the traditional approach to interviewing is modeled on the experiment as the ideal research method, the parallels are not surprising. In both endeavors the same strategy of concealment is adopted and investigators' aims, theories, and findings are hidden from subjects and respondents. Test procedures and questions on interview schedules restrict the range of possible responses to a predetermined set of categories reflecting an investigator's prior knowledge and interests. Investigators undertake their studies in a state of surprise anxiety, worried about whether their subjects will really be naive and whether they might do or say something that does not fit their preconceptions and thus make more difficult their analyses and interpretations. These features of mainstream research are notably and remarkably different from those found in studies in which the role relationship between interviewer and interviewee has been transformed, as in those described above. In the women's development project, for example, investigators are prepared to be surprised, are eager to communicate their findings, and rely for success of their work on interviewees' knowledge and experience rather than on their naiveté.

The relevance of these issues to the problem of the relation between scientific method and scientific knowledge is evident in Gergen's (1973) position "that social psychology is primarily an historical inquiry." Gergen questions the general assumption of the transhistorical validity of psychological laws and points, as Bakan does, to the paradox that although we want our work to be used, "we do not expect the utilization to affect the subsequent character of the function forms themselves" (p. 310). These expectations may be unjustified, in part because the language for presenting psychological knowledge is not value free but tends to be prescriptive, that it, it suggests positive ways of thinking and acting. Further, knowledge or "sophistication" regarding psychological principles may liberate people from the behavioral implications of these principles and the "laws" may not apply. "Knowledge increases alternatives to action, and previous patterns of behavior are modified or dissolved" (p. 313).

Gergen concludes that "the continued attempt to build general laws of social behavior seems misdirected, and the associated belief that knowledge of social interaction can be accumulated in a manner similar to the natural sciences appears unjustified. In essence, the study of social psychology is primarily an historical undertaking" (p. 316). Given the grounding of psychological laws in historical contexts and their changes over time, he suggests that the aim of scientific research should change from the search for general laws to efforts to sensitize persons to important factors that may affect behavior and thereby to increase the range of alternatives that they consider.

Gergen's (1978) critique of experimentation as the principal method in social-psychological research resonates closely with points I have made about standard interviewing practice. Noting the problem of the contextual "embeddedness" of social events, Gergen states: "In the attempt to isolate a given stimulus from the complex in which it is normally embedded, its meaning within the normative cultural framework is often obscured or destroyed. When subjects are exposed to an event out of its normal context they may be forced into reactions that are unique to the situation and have little or no relationship to their behavior in the normal setting" (p. 510). In his detailed analysis of research on the simple and widely accepted proposition that "attraction toward another is a positive function of O's similarity to P" (p. 517), that is, of similarity in attitudes, values, and traits between one's self and another person, Gergen is led to the conclusion that "all reasonable hypotheses are likely to be valid . . . there is no reasonable hypothesis about social activity that is not likely to contain truth value for at least some persons at some time" (p. 521). He asserts further that the "critical experiment" is expendable as a methodological strategy in the specific sense that it cannot provide a valid test of competing hypotheses.

Although there are some differences in emphasis between the

view I have been advancing about empowerment and Bakan's and Gergen's critiques of theoretical and methodological assumptions in psychological research we share an essential concordance. Their concern is still primarily with investigators' problems—how to develop more valid theories, how to design studies that are more sensitive to context. I have been emphasizing respondents' problems, that is, their efforts to develop adequate and coherent understandings of their experiences so that they may act more effectively for their own ends. Gergen's (1982) recent proposal for "generative theory" through which individuals will learn from research about alternative ways of thinking and acting is a form of empowerment, but it is more abstract than the studies described in this chapter that encourage individuals to change through their actual participation in a study. All of these various proposals for transforming the traditional, and largely unquestioned, relationship between researchers and subjects bring forward questions that merit serious attention and continued debate about the nature of scientific knowledge.[3]

In this chapter technical problems of research practice have been located in a larger sociopolitical context than is usual in, for example, studies of context effects restricted to variations in question order. I suggested that the decontextualization of experiences that is a principal feature of the mainstream approach to interviewing has wider cultural parallels. It is also apparent that there are close linkages between contextual issues, power differentials between investigators and their subjects, and conceptions about the nature and uses of scientific knowledge. The central question is whether and how different research practices and forms of interviewing may function to hinder or to facilitate respondents' efforts to construct meaning from their experiences, develop a fuller and more adequate understanding of their own interests, and act more effectively to achieve their purposes. The proposed transformations in research practice are intended to empower respondents by facilitating their efforts to learn and act.

Conclusion:
Prospects for Critical Research

This book mixes analysis with rhetoric. Evidence was assembled and arrayed along the structure of an argument. The basic premise of the argument is that the essential nature of interviewing as a form of discourse has been excluded from the dominant tradition of interview research. My intent has been to recover and to make explicit those special qualities of interviewing that mark it as a particularly strong method for research in the social sciences, to make them central components of a new model, and to show that systematic research can be conducted within this alternative perspective.

The discussion has been detailed and extended and, in bringing it to a close, I wish to be brief and avoid repetition and other common sins of concluding chapters, such as qualifying the force of an analysis with cautionary postscripts about its limitations or claiming too much for it through hyperbole. Within these strictures I will review the main themes and address some problems and prospects for the proposed radical change in interviewing practices.

The first step in the argument was to make problematic the underlying assumptions of the mainstream approach. Central to this approach is the definition of a research interview as a behavioral example of the stimulus-response model. This definition structures how investigators frame research questions and provides a set of technical procedures that have become habitual and routine. My task was to bring these assumptions and practices into question, argue the necessity for their reconsideration, and thereby open up the possibility for an alternative approach.

This task was undertaken through a critical review of research on interviewing. The general question addressed was whether results of interview studies support the theoretical and empirical requirements of the traditional model, particularly the requirement of standardization of meaning for questions and responses. I concluded that this requirement is demonstrably not satisfied in actual practice, that there is pervasive though unacknowledged variation in how questions are asked and what they and responses might mean, and that, in order to preserve the appearance of validity of these assumptions, ad hoc hypotheses and procedures are introduced into analyses and interpretations. Further, I argued that this failure is in principle not remediable within the framework of the underlying model because the model either neglects or distorts the principal characteristic of interviewing, namely, that it is a form of discourse.

This critique set the stage for an alternative approach. Interviews were redefined as speech events or speech activities, particular types of discourse regulated and guided by norms of appropriateness and relevance that are part of speakers' shared linguistic competences as members of a communtiy. Through this redefinition emphasis was placed on questioning and answering as forms of speech that are structured by these norms, rather than on questions and answers as decontextualized stimuli and responses. This approach allowed, indeed required, consideration of issues that are neglected, circumvented, or obscured by mainstream practices but are essential to the analysis and interpretation of interviews as discourse: the joint construction of the discourse by interviewees and interviewers, the prerequisite of an explicit theory of discourse and meaning for interpretation, and the contextual basis of meaning. In successive chapters each of these issues was elaborated and close attention was given to empirical materials, primarily transcripts of tape-recorded interviews.

In accord with this new perspective systematic methods for conducting and analyzing interviews were presented. For example, I showed that the interview schedule and interviewers' reports of responses are an inadequate and inaccurate record of the interview. In other words, the initial description of the "data" is seriously and irretrievably faulty; it cannot be corrected, nor can the actual discourse of the interview be recovered, by increasingly sophisticated coding procedures or statistical analyses. Rather, an accurate description, the basic requirement for reliable and valid analysis and interpretation, depends on tape recordings and careful transcription of interviews.

From transcriptions it becomes clear that the meanings of questions and answers are not fixed by nor adequately represented by the interview schedule or by code-category systems. Instead, meanings emerge, develop, are shaped by and in turn shape the discourse. Looking more closely at this process and focusing on the task faced by respondents as they try to answer questions in a coherent, relevant, and meaningful way, I found that under many different interviewing conditions their accounts often resemble stories, that is, they display narrative features. At this point I examined several systematic methods of narrative analysis. Finally, I expanded the concern with contextual effects in interviews to broader sociocultural issues and particularly to the impact on respondents of the typical asymmetric power relationship in interviews. I called this relationship into question and proposed alternative models intended to empower respondents, to facilitate their efforts to achieve a meaningful understanding of their experiences and act in the world in accord with their interests.

By focusing on methods and practices, for example, on the availability and feasibility of methods for narrative analysis, I have tried to keep the discussion close to the problems faced by investigators. I hoped also by this approach to make the point as clearly and strongly as possible that rejection of the mainstream tradition does not entail abandonment of interviewing as a method. Rather, my aim has been to reaffirm its distinctive strengths by showing that systematic research that is consistent with a reformulation of interviewing as a form of discourse is possible.

Both the proposed alternative and the earlier critique were presented in some detail. To avoid digressing from the primary focus on research practices, however, many issues were either not referred to or were noted in passing. I should like to take note of a few general questions in these closing remarks. First, where does my argument fit within the broader ongoing discourse on theory and method in the social sciences? Second, what factors may facilitate or impede movement of investigative work in the proposed direction? Third, what are some unresolved problems of the proposed alternative?

Although my inquiry into interviewing emerged from efforts to deal with problems in my own research, it developed against the background of a diverse and wide-ranging discussion of issues of theory and method in the social sciences. This discussion, contributed to by many commentators from many disciplines, reflects a sustained concern with the value of the received and dominant tradition, a model of science usually characterized by the term *positivism*. This concern is evidenced in articles and books on the "crisis" in anthropology, history, psychology, social psychology, and sociology and in frequent reference to the emergence of a "new paradigm." This is not the place for citation of an extensive literature (some of the issues are reviewed in an earlier article; Mishler, 1979), but one illustration may suggest the intensity and pervasiveness of the controversy.

In a recent review of a volume by the prominent sociologist W. G. Runciman on the philosophy of method in the social sciences, Lieberson (1984, p. 45) observes that the book deals with the "classic and ferocious" debate that has continued "without resolution for more than two hundred years" between those affirming and those denying "a fundamental difference in kind" between the natural and the social sciences. Runciman frames the debate as one between positivists, who recognize that human behavior is complex but see no obstacle in principle to the search for general laws and causal generalizations, and the proponents of a hermeneutic perspective. The latter view the contextually grounded meanings of human action as central and as requiring methods different from those in the natural sciences, that is, methods that are more appropriate to such questions as understanding the meaning of particular actions. Lieberson concludes that Runciman's proposal do not resolve these issues and that the debate will continue.

Clearly, my analysis of the special topic of interviewing uses this "classic" debate as a resource and in turn enters it on the side of interpretation. Issues of discourse, context, and meaning are central to my argument. I do not expect that one more contribution to this "ferocious" two-hundred-year-old controversy will resolve it. Indeed, the persistence of the debate serves as a reminder of a significant feature of social science research underplayed in my discussion, namely, that the mainstream approach is not monolithic.

For many experienced investigators the failings and inadequacies of standard methods documented in these pages will not be "news"; they are well aware of the deficiencies of traditional methods as well as the general debate. Nonetheless, as befits researchers, they are pragmatists. They are on the whole less interested in resolving philosophical issues than in solving, practically and efficiently, the difficult and recurrent problems of research. They want to get on with their work and to do it in a way that meets the criteria of their calling as scientists. I hope they will find this book useful, that it will encourage them in their own continued reflections on assumptions and practices, and that it may provide some additional justification for trying new approaches.

Models of interviewing, such as those contrasted in this book, are not disembodied ideas. In concentrating on methods and practices I have tried to show how these ideas are realized in actuality. In the dialectic of research, where a model guides and is expressed in practice, the latter in turn confirms and reinforces the model's assumptions. I have not discussed another significant feature of these relationships, which is that both models and practices are part of larger social and institutional frameworks of research. This system—of training institutions, professional organizations, academic departments, review committees, funding agencies, scientific journals—is the social field to which investigators are attentive and within which they make their way. How this social field is constituted markedly influences the direction of research.

Thus changes in a research model and its associated practices have potentially broad implications. Adopting a new approach entails obvious risks. How research is evaluated, how resources and rewards are distributed, and how these affect investigators' chances for success and advancement in their fields are intricately dependent on the current alignment of forces within the larger social field of inquiry. In referring throughout this book to the mainstream approach, I have implied that this alignment has taken a particular form. In pointing to the long-standing controversy about research in the social sciences, I am suggesting that the current form is not fixed or monolithic. There are countercurrents, strains within the social field. Investigators do face risks in pursuing a new direction of research, but it is important for them to know that they are not alone. Each new study enters into the debate. In changing their practices—suggesting new questions and theories, developing new methods, proposing new criteria of evaluation—investigators are also engaged in reshaping and realigning forces in the social and institutional context of research. In this way, perhaps, the problems of research scientists, who often find themselves pressed to conform to the dominant tradition, are similar to the problems of their research subjects. Having urged the adoption of practices that empower respondents, I am now suggesting that these practices may also empower researchers. In learning how to pursue their own theoretical and empirical interests in ways that connect them with rather than separate them from the larger collectivity, researchers may find their own experience of alienation reduced.

Finally, despite the rhetorical tone of this essay and the expository, relatively noncritical presentation of an alternative model, I do not view the proposed approach to interviewing as a panacea. Nor do I consider the specific methods discussed to be definitive. It is perhaps sufficient to point out that several possibilities were described at each step: different forms of transcription, various modes of narrative analysis, a range of new models for interviewee-interviewer relationships. This diversity marks the relative newness of this direction of work; widely accepted, standard methods have not emerged. I noted that I did not expect the triumph of one method as the preferred and dominant approach. The strength of this view of interviewing lies in the diversity that it welcomes and supports among models, questions, and methods about relations between discourse and meaning.

As work progresses criteria will develop within each subdomain of this family of approaches for assessing and evaluating the adequacy of particular studies. Questions about the objectivity, reliability, validity, and replicability of findings—the standard issues of scientific research—will continue to be asked, but answers will take a form consistent with the new perspective rather than with the outworn mainstream model. For example, the standard way of assessing the reliability of a coding system through a statistical index of agreement between coders does not address the problems involved in evaluating the usefulness of a form of typescript notation. Nor, to take another example, does the validity of an interpretation based on a particular model of narrative analysis depend simply on the correlation between the narrative structure, or some specified narrative feature, and some other variable external to the text itself. I am raising problems, not proposing solutions; as problems, they will come to be better understood through doing the work. It is important to recognize that solutions may bear little resemblance to those criteria and methods with which we are now familiar.

In a recent study of medical interviews (Mishler, 1984) I proposed a mode of inquiry called "critical research," which involves critical reflection on the assumptions underlying one's methods and research practices within a commitment to humane values. In that study my intent was to clarify the features of humane clinical practice and to develop a form of research that would promote such a practice. Specifically, my argument involved a critique of the biomedical model and the dominant voice of medicine combined with a counteremphasis on the patient's perspective, the aim being to recover and strengthen the voice of the lifeworld, that is, individuals' contextual understandings of their problems in their own terms. The view of interviewing recommended in this book, which urges the empowerment of respondents and proposes methods that respect their way of constructing meaning, which in other words is attentive to their voices, both extends and exemplifies this general approach to research.

Appendix:
Suggested Readings in
Narrative Analysis

In an essay on narrativity in historical writing, White (1980) observes:

> So natural is the impulse to narrate, so inevitable is the form of narrative for any report of the way things really happened, that narrativity could appear problematical only in a culture in which it was absent—absent or, as in some domains of contemporary Western intellectual and artistic culture, programmatically refused . . . Far from being a problem, then, narrative might well be considered a solution to a problem of general human concern, namely, the problem of how to translate *knowing* into *telling*, the problem of fashioning human experience into a form assimilable to structures of meaning that are generally human rather than culture-specific. (p. 5)

White's observation both reflects and helps to account for the extraordinary variety of scholarly traditions and approaches represented in the study of narratives. These traditions have long and complex histories, and references by commentators to Aristotle's *Poetics* as the starting point are not uncommon. With the important exceptions of historians and ethnographers, social scientists are Johnny-come-latelies to this endeavor. This lag may be accounted for by their "programmatic refusal" to attend to narrative because it does not fit easily within the dominant positivist culture of contemporary social science research. Signs of a change have already been brought to the attention of a wider public; a *New York Times Book Review* article, "Why Scholars Become Storytellers," refers to new directions of research among anthropologists, historians, psychologists, and sociologists, who "have become interested . . . in narrative structure, genre, and symbolic interpretation, once considered literature's domain," (Randall, 1984, p. 1).

The recent volume edited by Sarbin (1986) on *Narrative Psychology* is another significant sign of change, particularly in marking a new interest among psychologists in narrative. Bruner's (1986) collection of essays also reflects this development. Bruner emphasizes the distinctive role of narrative modes of thought in how cognitive understanding is arrived at and communicated.

In reviewing narrative-analytic methods I focused almost exclusively on interview studies and made only passing reference to work on other types of narrative. The latter include fiction, folktales, historical accounts, myths, conversational stories, and stories constructed for experimental study of cognition and memory. Problems faced in analyzing interview narratives are also addressed in various ways in these other areas of study. A preliminary guide to this literature may be helpful to other investigators in their work. Sources noted here are assembled from the unsystematic and contingent nature of my own reading in a relatively inexhaustible domain of inquiry; they should be viewed simply as starting points for further exploration.

Useful introductions to literary traditions of narrative study are Chatman (1980), who presents a framework for the analysis of narratives in different media, such as written fiction and film, based on combining traditions of American literary criticism and French structuralism; and Scholes and Kellogg (1966), who offer a comparative and historical perspective on different types of narrative. Culler's (1982) critical commentary on recent poststructuralist approaches is clear and instructive; he emphasizes the implications of the role assigned to the reader in construction and interpretation of texts. Jameson (1981), a Marxist literary critic, situates types of narratives and different models of narrative analysis within historical-political contexts. Lukács's (1971) essay "Narrate or Describe?" also examines different traditions of the novel for representing reality as these are related to larger socioeconomic structures and forces. An issue of *Critical Inquiry* (Autumn, 1980) devoted entirely to the study of narratives includes essays by investigators from different disciplines expressing different and often conflicting views. (See also in the Summer 1981 issue, "Critical Response.")

Rather than listing other sources in terms of discipline or type of narrative, I have arranged them in a way that is more directly relevant for empirical research on interviews. My comments and citations are brought together around four interrelated questions that investigators must address in their own studies.

1. What are the distinctive characteristics of narratives in comparison with other forms of text or discourse? In the last section of Chapter 4 I alluded to the differences between a view of the whole interview as a "story" and a view of interviews with particular stretches of material containing distinctive "stories" but having other types of discourse as well. This issue is omnipresent; it appears in all narrative-analytic traditions and with reference to all types of texts, and investigators take different stances toward it. We might view this distinction as a difference between an approach to narratives as paradigmatic, that is, as *the* way in which people transform "knowing into telling," as opposed to a view of narrative as one strategy or mode of telling. The dominant view is that narratives are one of many other forms.

Chatman (1981) succinctly summarizes the central "narratological" question as, "What is narrative per se?" (p. 802). He argues that narratives have a distinctive "logical structure" and that "narrative subsists in an event chain, operating through time" (p. 808). This general notion of temporal ordering, which we found in the Labov-Waletzky model of interview narratives, is a widely accepted minimal criterion. However, it is not strong enough to distinguish what we intuitively recognize as "stories" from other types of event sequences. White (1980), for example, argues that "true" historical narratives must have beginnings, middles, and endings and that early historical records, such as annals that include a list of dates and associated events in chronological order, are not narratives. Ricoeur (1981, pp. 278–279) makes a parallel point: "any narrative combines, in varying proportions, two dimensions: a chronological dimension and a non-chronological dimension . . . the activity of narrating does not consist simply in adding episodes to one another; it also constructs meaningful totalities out of scattered events. The art of narrating, as well as the corresponding art of following a story, therefore require that we are able *to extract a configuration from a succession* . . . This complex structure implies that the most humble narrative is always more than a chronological series of events."

The issue of whether more is required to make a story than a temporally connected sequence of events is a controversial one among cognitive psychologists working with story-grammar models. Wilensky's (1983) argument that a story must have a "point," and that this requisite feature is not captured by abstract structures such as story grammars, which simply link events and actions in their sequential order, is furiously debated in the open peer commentary to his article (see particularly, the comments by van Dijk, Lehnert, and Mandler; for an earlier version of this debate, see Black and Wilensky, 1979; Mandler and Johnson, 1980; and Rumelhart, 1980; also Mandler, 1984).

Developing a critique of the structuralist approach from the point of view of a narrative as a part of a "social transaction," Barbara Herrnstein Smith (1980, p. 232) presents a more relativistic view of "narrative discourse" as "not necessarily—or even usually—marked off or segregated from other discourse." Pointing out that our knowledge of past events is not usually narrative in structure and that most "stories" are not organized in a simple linear sequence, she proposes a much more general and less restricted definition. "We might conceive of narrative discourse most minimally and most generally as verbal acts consisting of *someone telling someone else that something happened.*"

The paradigmatic view of narratives referred to earlier is expressed most directly in recent reconceptualizations of theory and research in the fields of personality, human development, and psychoanalysis. Sarbin (1983), for example, proposes narrative as the "root metaphor" for psychology, because "human beings think, perceive, imagine, and make moral choices according to narrative structures" (p. 8). Cohler (1982, p. 207), addressing the problem of how individuals maintain a sense of coherence and consistency in their lives in the face of both expected and unexpected changes, discontinuities, and crises, asserts that "the personal narrative which is recounted at any point in the course of life represents the most internally consistent interpretation of past, experienced present, and anticipated future at that time." He argues further that because both the individual constructing his own narrative and others who respond to it have the same assumptions as to its necessary features, the analysis of narratives would be more appropriate to the study of human development than traditional methods of personality research. (See also McAdams, 1985, for a related application of a life-story approach to identity development.)

Schafer (1980, 1983) characterizes Freud's metapsychology as consisting of two narrative structures, one referring to development from the primitive libidinal stage to a state regulated by the ego and superego, and the second referring to the mental apparatus and its various mechanisms. Alternatively, he portrays "psychoanalytic dialogue in terms of two agents, each narrating or telling something to the other in a rule-governed manner" (1980, p. 34). In his view the analytic process is essentially a series of "retellings" of an analysand's stories. Schafer reinterprets such traditional psychoanalytic concepts as drives, free association, resistance, and reality testing as narrative structures. Stories are retold in different ways and at different times, depending on the particular issue that is being explored. "In this account, reality is always mediated by narration. Far from being innocently encountered or discovered, it is created in a regulated fashion" (p. 49). Consequently, "the primary narrative problem of the analyst is, then, not how to tell a normative chronological life history; rather it is how to tell the several histories of each analysis. From this vantage point, the event with which to start the model analytic narration . . . [is] the psychoanalyst's retelling of something told by an analysand and the analysand's response to that narrative transformation . . .

traditional developmental accounts . . . may now be seen in a new light: less as positivistic sets of factual findings about mental development and more as hermeneutically filled-in narrative structures" (p. 53). In making this contrast Schafer joins the debate I referred to between positivist and interpretive approaches in the human sciences.

A closely related position is developed by Spence (1982; see also Malcolm, 1983) in his discussion of criteria for "truth" in psychoanalytic interpretations. Spence argues that both patients and therapists are significantly influenced by their adherence to a "narrative tradition" in the production and interpretation of clinical data, such as memories, dreams, and experiences. "The form of these creative efforts is guided by the narrative tradition; as the vague outlines take on form and substance, they also acquire a coherence and representational appeal, which gives them a certain kind of reality. Narrative truth can be defined as the criterion we use to decide when a certain experience has been captured to our satisfaction; it depends on continuity and closure and the extent to which the fit of the pieces takes on an aesthetic finality . . . Once a given construction has acquired narrative truth, it becomes just as real as any other kind of truth; this new reality becomes a significant part of the psychoanalytic cure" (p. 31). He suggests that it may be more useful to view therapists as "pattern makers" rather than as "pattern finders."

Investigators with a paradigmatic orientation tend to be relatively inattentive to the question of whether there are different types of narrative; nor do they specify components, features, or modes of connection that enter into narrative structure. For example, Cohler, Schafer, and Spence assume but do not explicate the elements and assumptions of a "shared" understanding about *the* essential characteristics and structure of narratives. The same neglect of this issue is found among analysts of interview narratives who hold a view of the whole interview as a "story," such as Agar and Hobbs. When, alternatively, narratives are regarded as one among other modes or strategies of "telling," considerable emphasis is placed on specific features of narratives, how they vary among different types, and how they serve to distinguish narratives from other modes of discourse.

This is apparent in Labov's analyses of interview narratives and in the models proposed by van Dijk and Landau.

We find a similarly marked degree of attention to this problem in Chatman's (1980, p. 267) application of the structuralist approach; his diagrammatic representation of narrative structure includes more than twenty components with systematic relationships among them and various options among which a narrator may choose. At a more abstract level, White (1973, 1980) distinguishes among different historical narratives in terms of their general form of explanation by type of "emplotment," that is, "the way by which a sequence of events fashioned into a story is gradually revealed to be a story of a particular kind." He names the "kinds" of historical stories Romance, Comedy, Tragedy, and Satire. Specific narrative dimensions may also be selected for investigation, to ascertain variation under different conditions and context. For example, developmental psychologists have reported an age-related increase in the structural complexity of children's spontaneous narratives that parallels other linguistic and cognitive changes (Botvin and Sutton-Smith, 1977; Sutton-Smith, 1981; Sutton-Smith, Botvin, and Mahony, 1976). Focusing primarily on life stories of adolescent and adult development, Kenneth Gergen and Mary Gergen (1986; M. Gergen and K. Gergen, 1986) propose a typology defined by whether the stories indicate achievement of a desired state or goal: progressive, regressive, and stable narratives.

In sum, the answer an investigator gives to the question of whether a narrative is a distinctive or paradigmatic mode of discourse is consequential in significant ways for all aspects of a study.

2. What are the functions of narratives? "We tell ourselves stories in order to live" (Didion, 1979, p. 11). Didion's aphorism captures the deep seriousness and tragic undertone of storytelling. Turner (1980), an anthropologist, ascribes no less serious a function to narratives than does the essayist-novelist; he argues that they provide a way to articulate and resolve core, universal human problems so as to avoid cultural crises and discontinuities

and the disruption of social relationships. Relating the significance of narratives to cultural rituals and social dramas, the
latter viewed as universal social processes with four phases,
"breach, crisis, redress, and *either* reintegration *or* recognition of
schism" (p. 149), Turner states that narrative is "the supreme
instrument for binding the 'values' and 'goals' . . . which moti-
vate human conduct into situational structures of 'meaning,' "
and that "we must concede it to be a universal cultural activity,
embedded in the very center of the social drama" (p. 167).
Narrative functions specifically in situations of conflicting values
and interests; "the narrative component in ritual and legal action attempts to rearticulate opposing values and goals in a
meaningful structure, the plot of which makes cultural sense"
(p. 168).

Turner's analysis of the "binding" role of narratives, as well as
the work of other anthropologists concerned with relations between forms and functions of language, draws on the seminal
contributions of Lévi-Strauss in his studies of myth and social
organization. Lévi-Strauss (1963) asks us to "keep in mind that
mythical thought always progresses from the awareness of op-
positions toward their resolution" (p. 224) and that the "purpose of myth is to provide a logical model capable of overcoming
a contradiction (an impossible achievement if, as it happens, the
contradiction is real)" (p. 229).

Early (1982), another anthropologist, extends the range of
narrative functions from formal rituals and myths to the ways
that people try, through ordinary conversations in their daily
lives, to develop shared understandings of significant, recurrent
events, such as illnesses. She looks for the cultural patterning of
values in "therapeutic narratives," the "commentaries" in naturally occurring conversations on illness progression, curative
actions, and surrounding events . . . which are spontaneously
rendered and which, with time, are codified into an elaborated
version that is referenced and recounted for years to come" (p.
1491). She suggests that such narratives function like rituals and
ceremonies and that they employ "a web of commonsense explanations to link unique illness episodes with shared cultural
knowledge about illness" (p. 1494).

Charon (1985), a physician, medical educator, and writer, has used "stories" in a particularly innovative way in the diagnosis, treatment, and care of her patients. She refers to "stories and the imagination" as "instruments that allow us to see within our patients' lives" (p. 1) with a clarity equal to that achieved by medical instruments that allow physicians to see within their patients' bodies. She argues that medical work is "centered on telling stories and on hearing stories, and that by choosing one kind of story over another, we can transform our practice of medicine" (p. 4). When she is unclear about a patient's problems, she writes "stories" about them, filling in "with fiction the gaps there are in fact" (p. 5). Tying together the events and complaints in a patient's life, she also includes herself and tries to describe herself from the patient's point of view. Urging doctors to become "joyous," she suggests where "stories come in. The brutal and deadening aspects of medical training can be transformed into the most humanizing experience if we allow ourselves to come close to the stories" (p. 13).

Developmental and cognitive psychologists have addressed the functions of narratives for a wide variety of cognitive and linguistic skills and styles, for example: text comprehension (Rumelhart, 1975, 1977); learning and recall (Johnson and Mandler, 1980; Mandler and Johnson, 1977; Mandler, 1984); reading (Johnson, 1983); and literacy (Gee, 1985; Heath, 1982, 1983; Michaels, 1981, 1983, 1985; Michaels and Cazden, 1984). In studies of literacy investigators have been especially concerned with effects of different sociocultural contexts and their associated patterns of linguistic and cognitive socialization on children's literacy styles and competences, that is, on their ways of expressing meaning in and taking meaning from oral and written stories. Thus Heath (1982, p. 70) observes: "Children have to learn to select, hold, and retrieve content from books and other written or printed texts in accordance with their community's rules or 'ways of taking,' and the children's learning follows community paths of language socialization . . . The ways of taking employed in the school may in turn build directly on the preschool development, may require substantial adaptation on the part of the children, or may even run directly counter to aspects of the community's pattern."

Some of the implications of these differences are apparent in studies of how children tell stories in classrooms. Michaels (1981) distinguishes between "topic centered" and "topic associating" styles, the former more typical of white, middle-class children. Teachers find it difficult to follow, understand, and grasp the main point of a topic-associating story. When teachers "fail to hear the structure or logic in a child's discourse, they are naturally inclined (as we all are) to assume it isn't there; that the talk is rambling, unplanned, or incoherent" (Michaels and Cazden, 1984, p. 33; see also Gee's, 1985, analysis of the structure of an apparently "incoherent" story). This inability interferes with the degree to which teachers can participate in a dialogue with a child and "collaborate" in clarifying the meaning of what a child is trying to say. (See also Cazden, Michaels, and Tabors, 1984.)

The prominent lines of narrative research among cognitive psychologists focus on the structures of stories and their effects. Central to this work has been the development of "story grammars," in which formal constituents of texts and rules for their relationships are specified analogously to the syntactic structures and rules of sentence grammars, and "story schemata," which are generalized representations acquired through experience and learning of typical situations and events (Johnson, 1983; Mandler, 1984; Wilensky, 1983).

Rumelhart's (1975) "grammar," for example, includes syntactic and "semantic interpretation" rules that operate on such constituent elements as Setting, Episode, Event, and Reaction to generate a "string of sentences" in the form of a recognized story. In his studies of comprehension Rumelhart (1977, p. 269) characterizes problem solving as a basic "motif underlying a remarkable number of brief stories . . . Such stories have roughly the following structure: First, something happens to the protagonist of the story that sets up a goal for him to accomplish. Then the remainder of the story is a description of the protagonist's problem-solving behavior as he seeks to accomplish his goal" (p. 269). Rules and relationships specifying relationships between initiating event, goal, and attempt are referred to as an "episode schema." Rumelhart does not cite Propp, but the parallels between his motif-schema and the latter's underlying sequence of "functions" in fairy tales are evident; the similarity may reflect the general tendency for story-grammar researchers, including Rumelhart, to use folktales in their studies.

Ways that stories function in naturally occurring conversation have been explored by conversation analysts and ethnomethodologists. Sacks (1972) examines hearers' inferences and assumptions that allow them to interpret a sequence of utterances, in this case a pair, as a story; he also (1978) analyzes how speakers "package" their utterances so that listeners will know that a "story" is in process and that the speaker has a right to hold the floor for longer than usual. Applying the same perspective, Jefferson (1978b) shows how conversationalists insert or "fit" their stories into ongoing talk so as to articulate them without disruption with what came before and what comes after. Ryave (1978), also following this approach, looks at how conversationalists provide ways to relate to one another a "cluster" or series of successive stories.

Clearly the concept of function is manifold in its meanings and analytic uses. Halliday's triad of textual, ideational, and interpersonal functions, described in the text, represents one framework. The concepts of cultural and psychological functions radically enlarge the horizon of implications in the study of narratives. Their range and specification expands upon, perhaps transforms, and certainly differentiates further the set of "six basic functions" of language proposed in Jacobson's (1960) seminal paper: emotive, referential, poetic, phatic, metalingual, and conative. (See Robinson, 1972, pp. 49–56, for an expansion of this set.)

The functional significance of narratives is further extended by Dorothy E. Smith (1983), who focuses particularly on two accounts of the same event, "she committed suicide" and "she killed herself" (p. 309). Smith defines a "primary narrative" as "a telling of experience which intends, is grounded on and conforms itself to the lived actuality" (p. 325) and examines how a primary narrative is transformed into an "ideological form of narrative" that "depends upon the reader's or hearer's grasp of the appropriate interpretive schema of the professional or other textual discourse" (p. 328). The methods by which this transformation is accomplished are "ideological practices." These practices and the transformed narrative both express and sustain dominant orders of meaning, such as the psychiatric formulation of events in a person's life that is then used to "interpret" or "account for" "suicide." More generally these practices represent an objectified "form of social consciousness" and function to legitimate and preserve the interests of dominant, ruling groups and classes in hierarchically organized institutions and social systems. "Ideological practices . . . are functional constituents of a ruling apparatus" (p. 355).

I gave a novelist the first word in this discussion; the last word comes from another novelist: "Why are we huddling about the campfire? Why do we tell tales, or tales about tales—why do we bear witness, true or false? . . . Is it because we are so organized as to take actions that prevent our dissolution into the surroundings?" (Le Guin, 1980, p. 198).

3. How are narratives affected, in structure and specific features, by contexts and modes of expression? The pervasiveness of narrative forms is accompanied by the diversity of contexts in which they appear, and in which they have been studied. It is obvious, on intuitive and experiential grounds, that stories relayed through an oral tradition of folktales are different from those related in naturally occurring conversation; both of these differ from accounts elicited in life-history interviews; and all of these in turn differ from those accompanying a culturally charged ritual performance. It is equally evident that spoken and written narratives will differ from each other and from stories expressed in such nonlinguistic media as film and dance. Despite this variability detailed, comparative analyses across contexts and modes are rare. When attention has been directed to this issue, it has been to mode rather than context.

The relative neglect among interview researchers of various contextual effects on narratives, including the interviewee-interviewer relationship that I discussed in the text, is paralleled in other narrative analyses. This omission reflects both theoretical and empirical factors. On the whole, theory has focused on the most general, abstract features of narratives and addressed questions such as whether there is a universal structure for stories and how to distinguish stories from other types of discourse. Investigators tend to concentrate on a particular type of narrative expressed usually in one type of setting or context, for example, on folktales, written fiction, historical accounts, or classroom stories.

There are of course exceptions to this generalization. Hymes (1981), for example, centers much of his attention on the differences between the "story" told by an informant/narrator within the context of the ethnographic research relationship and the "story" sung or narrated within its culturally meaningful context, the latter conveyed by the concept of a "breakthrough into performance." This new "text" generates a form of analysis, "verse analysis," that moves interpretation closer to its cultural meaning. Barbara Herrnstein Smith (1980), in her critique of structuralist approaches to narratives as decontextualized entities, makes a strong case for the study of contexts by reconceptualizing narratives as "part of a social transaction" (p. 232). She argues that the particular features of a narrative are affected by the different motives, interests, and constraints involved in each storytelling situation, and that "the nature of the particular tale told" is a function of the "social and circumstantial context of the narrative and the structure of motivation that sustained the narrative transaction between the teller and his audience" (p. 234). This concern with context is evident in Paget's (1982) analysis of a physician's story of a medical error that he observed. Focusing on what she calls the "problematic of silence," Paget shows how this physician's silence, his failure to speak during the episode, and his efforts to account for what he did and did not do and say enter into the narrative work, that is, how they affect the way that he constructs the story in the interview.

Work on different modes of narrative expression is also noncontextual; that is, the principal concern is to find the "same" underlying story despite the different properties of different media through which "it" is represented. Thus Chatman (1978,

1980), using the structuralist two-level model of story as "what" is told and discourse as "how" it is told, shows how such features as the passage of time are communicated through different devices and strategies in film and text; in the former by flashbacks or dissolves, in the latter by verb tense. Occasionally, as in Smith's critique, this line of interpretation is challenged and questions are raised about the adequacy of these "translations" from one medium to another, or one language to another. Ong (1982), for example, asserts that interpretation of classic "texts," such as Homer's *Odyssey*, has relied too heavily on typical structures of written texts, thus neglecting the special characteristics of oral narratives, among them an episodic rather than a linear, temporal arrangement of events.

As social scientists become more actively engaged in studying narratives they are likely to bring to it their more general interests in contextual effects. Their special contributions to this cross-disciplinary domain of inquiry may be the analysis of how narratives are influenced by specific features of the "social and circumstantial context."

4. What is the relationship between a narrative and events in the world to which it refers? Each question I have discussed has a field of reference and a range of implications much beyond the limited scope and intent of this introductory guide. This last question, however, represents a quantum leap in order of complexity and in the degree to which its referential context may legitimately be said to include the history of all reflective discourse on human experience of the world, in short, on the profound questions of ontology. Clearly this is not the place to explore the deep meanings of these questions, but I may note here that investigators take a position, albeit often implicitly, on whether it is important to determine if a narrative "corresponds" to the "real" or "objective" world of events, to determine the nature, in Goodman's (1981, p. 799) phrase, of the "distinction between the order of the telling and the order of the told."

Naturally, the question of such correspondence in the sense of the "truth" of the narrative is not present in the same way in studies of fiction as it is in studies of other types of narrative; the category of fiction itself assures that other criteria are relevant to interpretation than a novel's veridicality. Consideration of other types of accounts, particularly those that purport to describe the world, must face the problem more directly. Even here, as is evident from earlier discussions, the narrative is often disconnected from its presumed world of objective reference and analyzed in its own terms. This is certainly true in Schafer's formulation of analyst-analysand reconstructions of life histories as "retellings" with the question of the "real" developmental course put aside, perhaps entirely outside the boundary of determinative interest. And it is also true of White's analysis of different types of historical accounts as varieties of "emplotment," for he is attentive primarily to the latter's narrative constraints.

Danto (1965) puts narrative, rather than the "true" representation of events, at the heart of historical inquiry. "To ask for the significance of an event, in the *historical* sense of the term, is to ask a question which can be answered only in the context of a *story*" (p. 11). Further, the use of narrative sentences linking two time-separated events marks "a differentiating feature of historical knowledge" (p. 43). For that reason, "narrative sentences offer an occasion for discussing, in a systematic way, a great many of the philosophical problems which history raises and which it is the task of the *philosophy* of history to try to solve . . . My thesis is that narrative sentences are so peculiarly related to our concept of history that analysis of them must indicate what some of the main features of that concept are" (p. 143).

Among investigators in the rapidly developing subfield of oral-history research there is a special interest in whether respondents' accounts are consistent with other historical data, such as official documents, diaries and journals, and other reports by observers at the time. Thompson (1978, 1981) makes the case for the importance of oral-history interviews and outlines specific steps for assessing "evidence" from diverse sources. Grele (1975a) and other contributors to his edited volume (1975b) also address this issue. (Examples of oral-history studies may be found in Bertaux, 1981b; Bertaux and Bertaux-Wiame, 1981a, b; Bertaux and Kohli, 1984; and Plummer, 1983.)

Applying models and concepts of story analysis to a setting in which the determination of "truth" is the primary aim, namely, courtroom testimony in legal suits and trials, Bennett and Feldman (1981) point to a major source of the difficulty in making such determinations in an unequivocal and definitive way; at the same time they suggest another reason for the pervasiveness of stories. Their observations apply equally to any account, in an interview or other setting, of "what" really happened.

> The importance of story structure stems from the fact that most social action is problematic. Almost any act can be associated with diverse causes, effects, and meanings . . . In addition to having the potential for multiple significance, social actions are so complex that exhaustive descriptions are impossible . . . Constructing an interpretation for a problematic social action . . . . requires the use of some communication device that simplifies the natural event, selects out a set of information about it, symbolizes the information in some way, and organizes it so that the adjudicators can make an unambiguous interpretation and judge its validity. Stories are the most elegant and widely used communication devices for these purposes.   (pp. 66–67)

Social scientists functioning within the long tradition of science and its special and distinctive responsibility to "search" for and "discover" truth cannot easily put aside or "relativize" the question of *the* truth of an account. This is widely recognized as a central issue in the controversial, historic debate I referred to earlier between the positivist and hermeneutic approaches to explanation. This issue remains unresolved, and its resolution is not in view. I find it worth closing, nevertheless, on a note that while not quite optimistic at least suggests that it may be possible, in those situations where it is relevant, both to do narrative analysis and to remain attentive to the world of real events. Scholes (1980), referring to Peirce's model for language analysis (1955), tries to break out of what Jameson (1972) refers to as the "prison-house of language" built by structuralist criticism, where everything but the words themselves are excluded from the field of attention and analysis, where "crudely, every word is defined by another word, in an endless chain which is hopelessly cut off from nonverbal affairs" (Scholes, 1980, p. 205).

Scholes argues that there has been a neglect of Peirce's emphasis on the "iconic" element in signs, the qualities of objects that they represent, as well as on their "indexical" properties, that is, on what they point to in the world. The process of encoding and decoding a story requires nonverbal information to ground its iconic and indexical meanings. "The object of a story is the sequence of events to which it refers; the sign of a story is the text in which it is told . . . and the interpretant is the . . . constructed sequence of events generated by a reading of the text" (p. 210). Scholes's comments on the distinction between and different rules governing fictional and historical narrative are applicable to those narratives in which social scientists are often interested, descriptions and reports of events: "The producer of a historical text affirms that the events entextualized did indeed occur prior to the entextualization. Thus it is quite proper to bring extratextual information to bear on those events when interpreting and evaluating a historical narrative" (p. 211). The accounts of personal experiences that we elicit in interviews are a type of "historical text." Scholes's observations supplement the argument advanced in this book that interpretation depends on the analyst's "expansion" of the interview narrative.

Notes

Introduction

1. The general point about the dependence of meaning on context and its implications for scientific research is developed in Mishler (1979). A fuller treatment of problems in the application of code-category systems is in Mishler (1984, chap. 2). Although the focus there is on coding observations of interaction, the same issues are present in coding interviewer responses. Garfinkel's (1967) discussion of coder's rules in the construction of clinic records remains a highly instructive analysis of the general problem.

2. These observations on survey interviewing, on both its dominance and its problems, are neither singular nor original. Many investigators, struggling against the relative hegemony of this approach as *the* scientific method, have made a similar point. To cite just one example here—others will serve as resources in the following chapters—Bertaux (1981b), arguing for the importance of life-history research in sociology, locates the dominance of survey interviewing and its associated quantitative procedures in the "positivistic" model of science. In discussing the choice of a method, he notes that "the question of technique selection is not a technical question. If, by 'social relations' we understand 'relations between variables,' we shall select the survey technique (actually, in using the concept of 'variable' at the theoretical level, *we have already chosen* the survey approach: or rather, it has chosen us). If, by 'social relations' we mean what the best theoreticians

mean, from Marx to Parsons, from Durkheim to Malinowski and Levi-Strauss, from Weber to the French structuralist and to Goffman, then we shall have to think it over a little" (pp. 35–36).

1. Standard Practice

1. These observations and the discussion that follows focus primarily on interviewing practices found in survey research, that is, on studies aimed at gathering information or determining attitudes from representative samples with the intent of generalizing findings to national or otherwise specified populations. This restriction of focus, however, does not limit the implications of the argument. The large majority of studies of particular institutions or subgroups in education, psychology, and sociology relies, often implicitly, on the same definition of the interview and of its aims. In addition, as I pointed out in the Introduction, this mainstream approach to interviewing serves as a standard for evaluating other types of interviewing.

It is important to note that although work of other investigators serves as the primary source material for the critique presented in this chapter, these ideas followed a more immanent course of development, which is to say that this analysis grew out of efforts to understand the problems and limitations of my own research interviews. The general argument made here applies equally to my own past work as well as to the work of others.

2. This distinction between language and behavior is elegantly and forcefully argued by Chomsky (1959) in his critique of Skinner's behavioral approach to linguistic development. The rules of discourse with which I am concerned are, of course, learned, whereas Chomsky is concerned primarily with innate, unlearned rules of grammar. Nonetheless, the comparison he makes between linguistic and behavioral definitions of language is directly relevant to the contrast I am making between the standard definition of interviewing as "verbal behavior" and the proposed alternative view of interviewing as a form of discourse.

3. Schuman and Presser's colleagues at the University of Michigan Institute for Social Research read the past differently. Cannell, Miller, and Oksenberg (1981, p. 392) assert that "question wording, an important determinant of the nature of the reporting task, has received considerable attention in the past four decades." These authors remark, however, on the decline of interest in another area to which their own attention is directed. "Despite the potential for interviewers

to bias data somehow, concern over interviewer effects has lessened in recent years" (p. 391). Clear assessment of research findings may be difficult when equally competent investigators disagree on whether or not a topic has been an object of study and interest.

4. This problem is not unique to survey research or other interviewing studies but is pervasive in the social and behavioral sciences. It is one consequence of the dominance of the positivist approach to theory and research. A general critique of this approach and discussion of context stripping as a problem may be found in Mishler (1979).

5. In a cogent critique of ethnographers' overreliance on interviewing in cultures where this form of speaking may not be a "well-established convention," Briggs (1983) concludes that "adequate applications of the interview technique and analyses of interview data presuppose a basic understanding of the communicative norms of the society in question" and that "ethnographic interviewing should emerge from a broader understanding of the communicative process" (p. 255).

6. Several readers of earlier drafts of this chapter noted my general lack of reference to the extant critical literature on the standard approach to interviewing. This section is, in part, a response to the comments of Sol Levine, Vicky Steinitz, and Susan Bell, who brought Luker's book to my attention, and Cathy Riessman, who referred me to Oakley's paper.

7. A recent report in the *APA Monitor* (the official newsletter of the American Psychological Association) suggests that the faults pointed out in this chapter are widely recognized, but do not shake the commitment of mainstream researchers to the survey approach. Rather, they intend to mount yet another "salvage" operation. Cordes (1985) summarizes the report of a seminar on "cognitive aspects of survey methodology" convened by the National Research Council's Committee on National Statistics with partial funding by the National Science Foundation (see Jabine et al., 1984). Seminar participants, eminent cognitive psychologists and survey researchers, refer to such problems in survey interviews as the following: the delicacy of questioning such that one word can change a question's meaning, the influence of responses to one item of responses to others, respondents' errors in recalling the time at which events occurred, respondents' uncertainty about the confidentiality of survey results and its effect on their willingness to be candid, the possibility that respondents are "put off" by the "dry non-interactive design" of standardized questions and the interviewer as a "neutral recording device," and that little is known about the influence on respondents' interpretations of questions of

Notes to Page 33 165

cultural and individual differences. Cordes cites one of the report's conclusions: "We simply do not know much about how respondents answer survey questions." These observations on problems echo those I have made in this chapter. Among the suggestions made to improve surveys is that they be "structured more like normal conversations" and that questionnaires be organized to parallel "the organization of the experience in memory." On the surface these recommendations are similar to mine, but they continue to ignore the central feature of interviewing as discourse and remain locked within the traditional framework of assumptions about interviewing. Again, technical solutions are offered for technical problems.

A comprehensive analysis of methodological problems in survey research with a series of recommendations for improving their quality and validity may be found in the two-volume study edited by Turner and Martin (1984). This work came to my attention too late for detailed citation, but the analysis of problems and approaches to their solution that are presented in considerable detail in this report of the Committee on National Statistics Panel on Survey Measurement of Subjective Phenomena appear to be closely congruent with the seminar report noted above. My criticism of that report thereby applies as well—this is a salvage operation and no fundamental reformulation of interviewing is proposed. Only a modest amount of attention is directed to the interview process, in contrast, for example, to extended presentations of statistical methods for assessing measurement error. Further, consideration of the nature of interviewing itself tends to be tacked on to the end of discussions of "technical" issues. One of the infrequent references to interviewing comes at the end of a chapter on "Why Do Surveys Disagree?" in a general section entitled "Nonsampling Sources of Variability." Turner (1984, vol. 2, p. 202) concludes his review by pointing to future directions: "We would also suggest that there is a need for a reconsideration of the assumptions that underlie the practice of survey research. The most fundamental phenomena of survey research are quintessentially social psychological in character. They arise from a complex interpersonal exchange, they embody the subjectivities of both interviewer and interviewee, and they present their interpreter with an analytical challenge that requires a multitude of assumptions concerning, among other things, how respondents experience the reality of the interview situation, decode the 'meaning' of survey questions, and respond to the social, presence of the interviewer and the demand characteristics of the interview. The burden of the observed anomalies should prompt a reconsideration of the social psychological foundations of survey research. The foregoing examples are indicative of the deficient state of our present knowledge. We doubt any instant solutions exist, but it seems clear that complacency will not suffice." It is clear that I have no quarrel with this recommendation. My work, presented in this book, is one attempt at such a reconsideration.

2. Research Interviews as Speech Events

1. Although my definition of interviews as speech events was anticipated by Wolfson (1976), my views differ sharply from hers. She concludes that unstructured interviews are not rule governed and hence are not speech events, whereas I think the evidence points overwhelmingly to the opposite conclusion. Wolfson's article was called to my attention by Theodore Sarbin after the first draft of this chapter was completed.

2. The selection of these interviews is in part a matter of necessity. Tape recording of field interviews is highly infrequent in mainstream studies and there is a scarcity of published transcripts providing sufficient detail for close analysis. In addition, the aim of this discussion is not the evaluation of interviewer performance. Rather, the intent is to make problematic the almost universal assumption that questions printed on an interview schedule and responses recorded by interviewers represent valid data adequate to the tasks of analysis and interpretation. I hope that using interviews from my own studies will underscore the point that the discrepancy found between assumed questions and responses and the actual discourse of interviewers and respondents is not primarily a technical issue of interviewer performance but an unavoidable feature of interviewing.

3. These observations on transcription are a preliminary introduction to a variety of issues that have been receiving increased attention with the recent expansion of research on naturally occurring speech by ethno- and sociolinguists, anthropologists, developmental psychologists, and ethnomethodologists. For a general discussion with examples of several different approaches, see Mishler (1984, chap. 2). Relationships between theoretical concerns, research problem, and transcript notation systems are evident through a comparison of the different methods found in the following reports, a focus on meaning units as speech units (Chafe, 1980); poetic forms of speech (Hymes, 1981); cultural differences in the organization and expression of thought (Scollon and Scollon, 1981; Tedlock, 1975, 1979, 1983); the

interactional organization of conversation (Jefferson, 1978a); forms of coherence in extended speech (Gee, 1985); affective cues (Labov and Fanshel, 1977); speaker differences and conflicts in meanings and intentions (Mishler, 1984).

3. The Joint Construction of Meaning

1. My judgment of the "irrelevance" of this story and its omission from the transcript presented here reflects my view at the time of the interview of the specific intent of this question for the general aims of the study. As I developed the alternative approach to interviewing presented in this book, I was led to reconsider the meaning and revelance of this respondent's story and to recognize its significance. I will return to the story in Chapter 4; a detailed analysis of its narrative structure and how it functions in the interview may be found in Mishler (1986).

2. An instructive analysis of the indexicality of language and the problems it poses for theory and research in the social sciences may be found in Garfinkel and Sacks (1970).

3. Vicky Steinitz brought this paper to my attention.

4. Language, Meaning, and Narrative Analysis

1. My initial interest in systematic analysis of interview narratives was stimulated by the studies, referred to in the text and the references, of Marianne Paget and Susan Bell. This chapter has changed considerably from earlier drafts, reflecting developments in my own work and a more extensive examination of the literature on narrative analysis as well as the suggestions and comments of many colleagues and friends.

2. The literature on narratives and their analysis is both diverse and voluminous. To avoid digression from the main topic and aim of this chapter, namely, analysis of interview narratives, I leave the discussion of some representative studies in various fields to the Appendix.

3. In particular I have had the good fortune to be permitted to listen to tapes and read transcripts of interviews conducted by W. Timothy Anderson, Susan Bell, Samuel D. Osherson, Marianne Paget, Catherine Riessman, Miles Shore, and Joseph Veroff.

4. A fuller and more systematic analysis of this story may be found in Mishler (1986) and will be reviewed near the end of this chapter.

5. The concept of interruption is introduced and developed in my study of medical interviews (Mishler, 1984), where I show how physi-

cians routinely and typically interrupt patients' stories through their control of the form and content of a medical interview. Although research interviews differ from medical interviews in many respects, researchers tend to interrupt respondents' stories through their predetermination of the order of standard questions in interview schedules and their on-the-spot decisions on when enough has been said to serve as an adequate and relevant response.

6. Halliday's triad of functions is a useful framework for describing the features and consequences of different approaches, and I have used it before (see Mishler, 1984). My application of his categories is highly restricted and does not represent his systematic and comprehensive theory of language.

7. Labov's neglect of interviewer effects in his studies of narratives is unusual and puzzling given that a significant contribution of his studies of Black English was his emphasis on the effects of interviewer characteristics and interview contexts. See the studies in Labov, 1972a.

8. It is worth noting in this context that even when an investigator draws directly on the Labov-Waletzky framework the relationship of temporal ordering between events and narrative is only of peripheral interest. Examining how stories reveal cultural presuppositions and values; Polanyi (1981, p. 100) uses Labov's distinction between narrative and nonnarrative clauses, relabeling them as clauses carrying "event information" or "durative-descriptive information," as well as his category of evaluation. She constructs "paraphrases," at different levels of adequacy, of a story told in conversation. The significant point for the present discussion is that these paraphrasings are based on a speaker's evaluations of the importance of different parts of the account and refer to both event and durative-descriptive information, without distinction as to their respective values for interpretation. The temporal ordering of events and clauses plays no appreciable role in her analysis. Polanyi (1985) has applied her method of narrative analysis, focused on the interpretation of "adequate paraphrases," to the study of core American values as they are expressed in stories told in conversations.

9. Yet another approach to coherence, drawing on methods of literary criticism and differing from both Agar and Hobbs and van Dijk, is presented by Gee (1985) in his analysis of a child's story told in school. Gee's structural analysis focuses on how the child groups her lines into stanzas that in turn serve narrative functions. Gee then argues that the text achieves "overall coherence and structure" through "technical devices" that are familiar in poetry and literature, such as

"repetition, parallelism, sound play, juxtaposition, foregrounding, delaying, and showing rather than telling" (p. 26).

10. Bell's permission to refer to and cite her unpublished study is gratefully acknowledged.

11. The story-grammar approach is described in the Appendix.

12. The wide range of interests that may be served through narrative analysis will be apparent in the Appendix, where work is reviewed on types of narratives other than those occurring in interviews. All of the approaches described in this chapter and the Appendix are directed to the analysis of individual narratives. Approaches to life-history interviews that place more emphasis on the comparability of accounts within and across subgroups, on formal methods of classification and measurement, and on procedures for aggregate data analysis are reviewed in Carr-Hill and Macdonald (1973) and Tagg (1985).

13. Tagg's analysis of potential sources of error in life-story interviews and his suggestions of ways to control for them may be supplemented by guidelines proposed by investigators who focus on other stages of a study. For example, with regard to the problem of sampling Bertaux and Bertaux-Wiame (1981a) suggest an alternative to the usual type of "representative" sample; they "conducted interviews . . . until we felt new interviews were not bringing us any new knowledge about the level of social relations . . . a process of saturation . . . all interviews gave the same results . . . This process of saturation of knowledge means that we get a certain representativeness indeed, not at the level of the phenomena, but at the level of social relations which produce them everywhere" (p. 179). Charmaz (1983) outlines successive phases in coding observations, from initial through focused codes, giving attention to the complex interplay between data collection and analysis. Katz (1983) emphasizes the search for negative instances that do not fit prior interpretations, and the role they play in the development and reshaping of interpretations. Thompson (1978), an oral historian, discusses how external sources of evidence—documents, administrative records, reports of on-the-scene observers—may be used to evaluate the accuracy of respondents' accounts of historical events. Gittins (1979), also an oral historian, describes ways of determining the degree of representativeness of a current sample of respondents for the earlier population to which the data are intended to refer. The comparative analysis of life histories may require quantification and statistical analysis; Carr-Hill and Macdonald (1973) and Tagg (1985) present several approaches to these problems.

5. Meaning in Context and the Empowerment of Respondents

1. This position for empowering respondents parallels the argument for the empowerment of patients developed in my study of medical interviews (Mishler, 1984). In both instances the intent is to reorient practices so as to reduce the asymmetry of power and to restore a measure of autonomy and control to, respectively, research subjects and patients.

2. Ethnographic work is not immune from the problem discussed here of the relation between scientific and "native" theories. Karp and Kendell's (1982, p. 269) description of the tension between theories has the additional merit of locating anthropologists within the context of their discipline: "anthropologists' accounts face in two directions. On the one hand they must be faithful to the members of the society that is being studied, and on the other hand they must conform to the criteria of the scientific community of which the anthropologist is a member. This is not an easy task. All too often the delicate balance is lost. That the scale tips in favor of the scientific community in most cases and not in favor of the natives may tell us something about the relative balance of power in the world. That anthropologists justify the obliteration of meaning from their accounts on the grounds of the logic of validation may tell us something about the triumph of an ideology of technical rationality." (For another example of the "triumph of the ideology of technical rationality" in the clinical practice of medicine, see Mishler, 1984.)

3. These aims, of empowerment or of sensitizing individuals to alternative possibilities, are related to Rosenwald's (1985) proposal that the essential criterion for a study be the "enhancement" of subjects, that is, a deeper understanding of their problems that permits more effective resolution and action.

References

Agar, Michael. 1979. "Themes Revisited: Some Problems in Cognitive Anthropology." *Discourse Processes* 2:11–31.

———. 1980. "Stories, Background Knowledge, and Themes: Problems in the Analysis of Life History Narrative." *American Ethnologist* 7:233–239.

Agar, Michael, and Jerry R. Hobbs. 1982. "Interpreting Discourse: Coherence and the Analysis of Ethnographic Interviews." *Discourse Processes* 5:1–32.

———. 1983. "Natural Plans: Using AI Planning in the Analysis of Ethnographic Interviews." *Ethos* 11 (nos. 1/2): 33–48.

Bakan, David. 1967. *On Method: Toward a Reconstruction of Psychological Investigation.* San Francisco: Jossey-Bass.

Belenky, Mary Field, Blythe Clinchy, Nancy Goldberger, and Jill Mattuck Turule. 1981–82. "Listening to Women's Voices." *Newsletter, Education for Women's Development Project*, no. 2. Great Barrington, Mass.: Simon's Rock of Bard College.

Bell, Susan. "Narratives of Health and Illness I: DES Daughters Tell Stories." Unpublished paper.

Bennett, W. Lance, and Martha S. Feldman. 1981. *Reconstructing Reality in the Courtroom.* New Brunswick, N.J.: Rutgers University Press.

Benney, Mark, and Everett C. Hughes. 1956. "Of Sociology and the Interview." *American Journal of Sociology* 62:137–142.

Bertaux, Daniel. 1981a. "From the Life-History Approach to the

Transformation of Sociological Practice." In *Biography and Society: The Life History Approach in the Social Sciences,* ed. Daniel Bertaux. Beverly Hills, Calif.: Sage.

————, ed. 1981b. *Biography and Society: The Life History Approach in the Social Sciences.* Beverly Hills, Calif.: Sage.

Bertaux, Daniel, and Isabelle Bertaux-Wiame. 1981a. "Artisanal Bakery in France: How It Lives and Why It Survives." In *The Petite Bourgeoisie: Comparative Studies of the Uneasy Stratum,* ed. Frank Bechofer and Brian Elliott. New York: St. Martin's Press.

————. 1981b. "Life Stories in the Bakers' Trade." In *Biography and Society: The Life History Approach in the Social Sciences,* ed. Daniel Bertaux. Beverly Hills, Calif.: Sage.

Bertaux, Daniel, and Martin Kohli. 1984. "The Life Story Approach: A Continental View." *Annual Review of Sociology* 10:215–237.

Beza, Angell. 1984. "Review Essay: Experiments within Surveys." *Contemporary Sociology* 13:35–37.

Black, J. G., and R. Wilensky. 1979. "An Evaluation of Story Grammars." *Cognitive Science* 3:213–230.

Botvin, Gilbert J., and Brian Sutton-Smith. 1977. "The Development of Structural Complexity in Children's Fantasy Narratives." *Developmental Psychology* 13:377–388.

Bradburn, Norman M., and Seymour Sudman. 1979. *Improving Interview Method and Questionnaire Design.* San Francisco: Jossey-Bass.

Brenner, Michael. 1982. "Response Effects of "Role-restricted' Characteristics of the Interviewer." Chapter 5 in *Response Behavior in the Survey Interview,* ed. W. Dijkstra and J. van der Zouwen. New York: Academic Press.

————. 1985. "Survey Interviewing." In *The Research Interview: Uses and Approaches,* ed. Michael Brenner, Jennifer Brown, and David Canter. New York: Academic Press.

————, ed. 1981. *Social Method and Social Life.* New York: Academic Press.

Brenner, Michael, Jennifer Brown, and David Canter, eds. 1985. *The Research Interview: Uses and Approaches.* New York: Academic Press.

Briggs, Charles L. 1983. "Questions for the Ethnographer: A Critical Examination of the Role of the Interview in Fieldwork." *Semiotica* 46:233–261.

————. 1984. "Learning How to Ask: Native Metacommunicative Competence and the Incompetence of Fieldwork." *Language in Society* 13:1–28.

Brown, Jennifer, and Jonathan Sime. 1981. "A Methodology for Accounts." In *Social Method and Social Life,* ed. Michael Brenner. New York: Academic Press.

Bruner, Jerome. 1986. *Actual Minds, Possible Worlds.* Cambridge, Mass.: Harvard University Press.

Campbell, Donald T. 1979. " 'Degrees of Freedom' and the Case Study." In *Qualitative and Quantitative Methods in Evaluation Research,* ed. Thomas D. Cook and Charles S. Reichardt. Beverly Hills, Calif.: Sage.

Campbell, Donald T., and Julian C. Stanley. 1963. "Experimental and Quasi-Experimental Designs in Educational Research." Chapter 5 in *Handbook of Research on Teaching,* ed. N. L. Gage. Chicago: Rand McNally.

Cannell, Charles F., Sally A. Lawson, and Doris L. Hausser. 1975. *A Technique for Evaluating Interviewer Performance.* Ann Arbor: Survey Research Center of the Institute for Social Research, University of Michigan.

Cannell, Charles F., Peter V. Miller, and Lois Oksenberg. 1981. "Research on Interviewing Techniques." Chapter 11 in *Sociological Methodology,* ed. Samuel Leinhardt. San Francisco: Jossey-Bass.

Carr-Hill, R. A., and K. I. Macdonald. 1973. "Problems in the Analysis of Life Histories." In *Stochastic Processes in Sociology,* ed. R.E.A. Mapes, special issue. *Sociological Review,* monograph no. 19:57–95.

Cazden, Courtney B., Sarah Michaels, and Patton Tabors. 1984. "Spontaneous Repairs in Sharing Time Narratives: The Intersection of Metalinguistic Awareness, Speech Event, and Narrative Style." In *The Acquisition of Written Language: Revision and Response,* ed. S. M. Freedman. Norwood, N.J.: Ablex.

Chafe, W. L., ed. 1980. *The Pear Stories: Cognitive, Cultural and Linguistic Aspects of Narrative Production.* Norwood, N.J.: Ablex.

Charmaz, Kathy. 1983. "The Grounded Theory Method: An Explication and Interpretation." In *Contemporary Field Research: A Collection of Readings,* ed. Robert M. Emerson. Boston: Little Brown.

Charon, Rita. 1985. Commencement address, State University of New York, Stony Brook School of Medicine, June. Unpublished.

Chatman, Seymour. 1978. *Story and Discourse: Narrative Structure in Fiction and Film.* Ithaca, N.Y.: Cornell University Press.

———. 1980. "What Novels Can Do That Films Can't (and Vice Versa)." *Critical Inquiry* 7:121–140.

———. 1981. "Critical Response: Reply to Barbara Herrnstein Smith." *Critical Inquiry* 7:802–809.

Chomsky, Noam. 1959. "Review of *Verbal Behavior* by B. F. Skinner

(New York: Appleton-Century-Crofts, 1957)." *Language* 35 (no. 4):26–58.

Cicourel, Aaron V. 1967. "Fertility, Family Planning, and the Social Organization of Family Life: Some Methodological Issues." *Journal of Social Issues* 23 (no. 4):57–81.

———. 1982. "Interviews, Surveys, and the Problem of Ecological Validity." *American Sociologist* 17:11–20.

Cohler, Bertram J. 1982. "Personal Narrative and Life Course." In *Life-Span Development and Behavior.* vol. 4, ed. Paul B. Baltes and Orville G. Brim, Jr. New York: Academic Press.

Connell, R. W., and Murray Goot. 1972–73. "Science and Ideology in American 'Political Socialization' Research." *Berkeley Journal of Sociology* 27:166–193.

Cook, Thomas D., and Donald T. Campbell. 1979. *Quasi-Experimentation: Design and Analysis Issues for Field Settings.* Chicago: Rand McNally.

Cordes, Colleen. 1985. "Fields Cooperate to Study Surveys." *APA Monitor* 16 (no. 6):32.

Critical Inquiry. 1980. "On Narrative." 7:1–236.

Critical Inquiry. 1981. "Critical Response." 7:777–809.

Cronbach, Lee J. 1982. *Designing Evaluations of Educational and Social Programs.* San Francisco: Jossey-Bass.

Cronbach, Lee J., and associates. 1980. *Toward Reform of Program Evaluation.* San Francisco: Jossey-Bass.

Cronbach, Lee J., Goldine C. Gleser, Harinda Nanda, and Nageswari Rajaratnam. 1972. *The Dependability of Behavioral Measurements: Theory of Generalizability for Scores and Profiles.* New York: Wiley.

Cronbach, Lee J., and Paul E. Meehl. 1955. "Construct Validity in Psychological Tests." *Psychological Bulletin* 52:281–302.

Culler, Jonathan. 1982. *On Deconstruction: Theory and Criticism after Structuralism.* Ithaca, N.Y.: Cornell University Press.

Danto, Arthur C. 1965. *Analytical Philosophy of History.* Cambridge: Cambridge University Press.

DeLamater, John. 1982. "Response-effects of Question Content." Chapter 2 in *Response Behavior in the Survey Interview,* ed. W. Dijkstra and J. van der Zouwen. New York: Academic Press.

Didion, Joan. 1979. *The White Album.* New York: Simon and Schuster.

van Dijk, Teun A. 1977. "Semantic Macro-Structures and Knowledge Frames in Discourse Comprehension." In *Cognitive Processes in Comprehension,* ed. M. A. Just and P. A. Carpenter. Hillsdale, N.J.: Lawrence Erlbaum Associates.

————. 1980. *Macrostructures: An Interdisciplinary Study of Global Structures in Discourse, Interaction, and Cognition.* Hillsdale, N.J.: Lawrence Erlbaum Associates.

————. 1982. "Episodes as Units of Discourse Analysis." In *Analyzing Discourse: Text and Talk,* ed. Deborah Tannen. Washington, D.C.: Georgetown University Press.

————. 1983. "A Pointless Approach to Stories." *Behavioral and Brain Sciences* 6:598–599.

Dijkstra, Wil, Lieneke van der Veen, and Johannes van der Zouwen. 1985. "A Field Experiment on Interviewer-Respondent Interaction." In *The Research Interview: Uses and Approaches,* ed. Michael Brenner, Jennifer Brown, and David Canter. New York: Academic Press.

Dijkstra, W., and J. van der Zouwen, eds. 1982. *Response Behavior in the Survey Interview.* New York: Academic Press.

Dillon, J. T. 1981. "Categories of Literature on Questioning in Various Enterprises: An Introduction and Bibliography." *Language Sciences* 3:337–358.

————. 1982. "The Multidisciplinary Study of Questioning." *Journal of Educational Psychology* 74:147–165.

Early, Evelyn. 1982. "The Logic of Well Being: Therapeutic Narratives in Cairo, Egypt." *Social Science and Medicine* 16:1491–1497.

Erikson, Kai T. 1976. *Everything in Its Path: Destruction of Community in the Buffalo Creek Flood.* New York: Simon and Schuster.

Florio, Susan, and Martha Walsh. 1981. "The Teacher as Colleague in Classroom Research." In *Culture and the Bilingual Classroom: Studies in Classroom Ethnography,* ed. Henry T. Trueba, Grace P. Guthrie, and Kathryn H. Au. Rowley, Mass.: Newbury House.

Frake, Charles O. 1964. "Notes on Queries in Ethnography." In *Transcultural Studies in Cognition,* ed. A. K. Romney and R. G. D'Andrade, special issue. *American Anthropologist* 66 (no. 3, pt. 2): 132–145.

————. 1977. "Plying Frames Can Be Dangerous: Some Reflections on Methodology in Cognitive Anthropology." *Quarterly Newsletter of the Institute for Comparative Human Development* 1 (no. 3):1–7.

Freire, Paulo. 1970. *Pedagogy of the Oppressed.* New York: Herder and Herder.

Garfinkel, Harold. 1956. "Conditions of Successful Degradation Ceremonies." *American Journal of Sociology* 61:420–424.

————. 1967. *Studies in Ethnomethodology.* Englewood Cliffs, N.J.: Prentice-Hall.

Garfinkel, Harold, and Harvey Sacks. 1970. "On Formal Structures of Practical Actions." In *Theoretical Sociology: Perspectives and Development,* ed. J. C. McKinney and E. A. Tiryakian. New York: Appleton-Century-Crofts.

Gee, James P. 1985. "The Narrativization of Experience in the Oral Style." *Journal of Education* 167:9–35.

Gergen, Kenneth J. 1973. "Social Psychology as History." *Journal of Personality and Social Psychology* 26:309–320.

———. 1978. "Experimentation in Social Psychology: A Reappraisal." *European Journal of Social Psychology* 8:507–527.

———. 1982. *Toward Transformation in Social Knowledge.* New York: Springer-Verlag.

Gergen, Kenneth J., and Mary Gergen. 1986. "Narrative Form and the Construction of Psychological Theory." In *Narrative Psychology: The Storied Nature of Human Conduct,* ed. Theodore R. Sarbin. New York: Praeger.

Gergen, Mary M., and Kenneth J. Gergen. 1986. "The Social Construction of Narrative Accounts." In *Historical Social Psychology,* ed. Kenneth J. Gergen and Mary Gergen. Hillsdale, N.J.: Lawrence Erlbaum Associates, forthcoming.

Gilligan, Carol. 1982. *In a Different Voice.* Cambridge, Mass.: Harvard University Press.

Gittins, Diana. 1979. "Oral History, Reliability, and Recollection." In *The Recall Method in Social Surveys,* ed. Louis Moss and Harvey Goldstein. London: University of London Institute of Education.

Glaser, Barney G., and Anselm L. Strauss. 1967. *The Discovery of Grounded Theory: Strategies for Qualitative Research.* Chicago: Aldine.

Goffman, Erving. 1961. *Asylums.* New York: Anchor Books.

———. 1976. "Replies and Responses." *Languages in Society* 5:257–313.

Goodman, Nelson. 1980. "Twisted Tales; or Story, Study, and Symphony." *Critical Inquiry* 7:103–119.

———. 1981. "Critical Response: The Telling and the Told." *Critical Inquiry* 7:799–801.

Grele, Ronald J. 1975a. "Movement without Aim: Methodological and Theoretical Problems in Oral History." In *Envelopes of Sound,* ed. Ronald J. Grele. Chicago: Precedent Publishing.

———, ed. 1975b. *Envelopes of Sound.* Chicago: Precedent Publishing.

Gumperz, John J. 1982. *Discourse Strategies.* Cambridge: Cambridge University Press.

Hagenaars, Jacques A., and Ton G. Heinen. 1982. "Effects of Role-independent Interviewer Characteristics on Responses." Chapter

4 in *Response Behavior in the Survey Interview,* ed. W. Dijkstra and J. van der Zouwen. New York: Academic Press.

Halliday, M. A. K. 1970. "Language Structure and Language Function." In *New Horizons in Linguistics,* ed. J. Lyons. Harmondsworth: Penguin Books.

———. 1973. *Explorations in the Functions of Language.* London: Edward Arnold.

Halliday, M. A. K., and R. Hasan. 1976. *Cohesion in English.* London: Longman.

Heath, Shirley Brice. 1982. "What No Bedtime Story Means: Narrative Skills at Home and School." *Language in Society* 11:49–76.

———. 1983. *Ways with Words: Language, Life, and Work in Communities and Classrooms.* Cambridge: Cambridge University Press.

Hobbs, Jerry R. 1978. "Why Is Discourse Coherent?" *Technical Note,* no. 176. Menlo Park, Calif.: SRI International.

———. 1979. "Coherence and Coreference." *Cognitive Science* 3:67–90.

Hobbs, Jerry R., and Michael Agar. 1981. "Text Plans and World Plans in Natural Discourse." *Proceedings, International Joint Conference on Artificial Intelligence,* pp. 190–196.

Hobbs, Jerry R., and Jane J. Robinson. 1979. "Why Ask?" *Discourse Processes* 2:311–318.

Hyman, Herbert. 1955. *Survey Design and Analysis: Principles, Cases and Procedures.* Glencoe, Ill.: Free Press.

Hymes, Dell. 1967. "Models of the Interaction of Language and Social Setting." *Journal of Social Issues* 33 (no. 2):8–28.

———. 1972. "Models of the Interaction of Language and Social Life." Chapter 1 in *Directions in Sociolinguistics,* ed. John J. Gumperz and Dell Hymes. New York: Holt, Rinehart, and Winston.

———. 1981. *"In Vain I Tried to Tell You."* Philadelphia: University of Pennsylvania Press.

Jabine, Thomas B., Miron L. Straf, Judith M. Tanur, and Roger Tourangeau. 1984. *Cognitive Aspects of Survey Methodology: Building a Bridge between Disciplines.* Washington, D.C.: National Academy Press.

Jacobson, Roman. 1960. "Closing Statement: Linguistics and Poetics." In *Style in Language,* ed. Thomas A. Sebeok. Cambridge, Mass.: MIT Press.

Jameson, Fredric. 1972. *The Prison-House of Language: A Critical Account of Structuralism and Russian Formalism.* Princeton, N.J.: Princeton University Press.

———. 1981. *The Political Unconscious: Narrative as a Socially Symbolic Act.* Ithaca, N.Y.: Cornell University Press.

Jefferson, Gail. 1978a. "Explanation of Transcript Notation." In *Studies in the Organization of Conversational Interaction*. ed. Jim Schenkein. New York: Academic Press.

———. 1978b. "Sequential Aspects of Storytelling in Conversation." Chapter 9 in *Studies in the Organization of Conversational Interaction,* ed. Jim Schenkein. New York: Academic Press.

Johnson, Nancy S. 1983. "There's More to a Story Than Meets the Eye: The Role of Story Structure and Story Schemata in Reading." Paper presented at the University of Wisconsin Symposium on Factors Related to Reading Performance.

Johnson, Nancy S., and Jean M. Mandler. 1980. "A Tale of Two Structures: Underlying and Surface Forms in Stories." *Poetics* 9:51–86.

de Joia, Alex, and Adrian Stenton. 1980. *Terms in Systemic Linguistics: A Guide to Halliday.* New York: St. Martin's Press.

Just, Marcel A., and Patricia A. Carpenter, eds. 1977. *Cognitive Processes in Comprehension.* Hillsdale, N.J.: Lawrence Erlbaum Associates.

Kahn, Robert L., and Charles F. Cannell. 1957. *The Dynamics of Interviewing: Theory, Technique, and Cases.* New York: Wiley.

Karp, Ivan, and Martha B. Kendall. 1982."Reflexivity in Field Work." In *Explaining Human Behavior.* ed. Paul F. Secord. Beverly Hills, Calif.: Sage.

Katz, Jack. 1983. "A Theory of Qualitative Methodology: The Social System of Analytic Fieldwork." In *Contemporary Field Research,* ed. Robert M. Emerson. Boston: Little, Brown.

Kidder, Louise H. 1981. *Research Methods in Social Relations,* 4th ed. New York: Holt, Rinehart and Winston.

Kintsch, Walter. 1977. "On Comprehending Stories." In *Cognitive Processes in Comprehension,* ed. M. A. Just and P. A. Carpenter. Hillsdale, N.J.: Lawrence Erlbaum Associates.

Kohlberg, Lawrence. 1969. "Stage and Sequence: The Cognitive-Developmental Approach to Socialization." In *Handbook of Socialization Theory and Research,* ed. D. A. Goslin. Chicago: Rand McNally.

Kohlberg, Lawrence, and R. Kramer. 1969. "Continuities and Discontinuities in Child and Adult Moral Development." *Human Development* 12:93–120.

Labov, William. 1972a. *Language in the Inner City: Studies in the Black English Vernacular.* Philadelphia: University of Pennsylvania Press.

———. 1972b. "The Transformation of Experience in Narrative Syntax." In *Language in the Inner City: Studies in the Black English*

Vernacular, ed. William Labov. Philadelphia: University of Pennsylvania Press.

———. 1982. "Speech Actions and Reactions in Personal Narrative." In *Analyzing Discourse: Text and Talk,* ed. Deborah Tannen. Washington, D.C.: Georgetown University Press.

Labov, William, and David Fanshel. 1977. *Therapeutic Discourse: Psychotherapy as Conversation.* New York: Academic Press.

Labov, William, and Joshua Waletzky. 1967. "Narrative Analysis: Oral Versions of Personal Experience." In *Essays on the Verbal and Visual Arts,* ed. June Helms. Seattle: University of Washington Press.

Landau, Misia. 1984. "Human Evolution as Narrative." *American Scientist* 72:262–268.

———. 1986. "Grafton Elliot Smith and the Temple of Doom." In *Narrative Psychology: The Storied Nature of Human Conduct,* ed. Theodore R. Sarbin. New York: Praeger.

Laslett, Barbara, and Rhona Rapoport. 1975. "Collaborative Interviewing and Interactive Research." *Journal of Marriage and the Family,* pp. 968–977.

Lazarsfeld, Paul. 1935."The Art of Asking Why: Three Principles Underlying the Formulation of Questionnaires." *National Marketing Review* 1 (no. 1):1–7.

Le Guin, Ursula K. 1980. "It Was a Dark and Stormy Night; or, Why Are We Huddling about the Campfire." *Critical Inquiry* 7:191–199.

Lévi-Strauss, Claude. 1963. *Structural Anthropology.* New York: Basic Books.

Levy, Philip, 1981. "On the Relation between Method and Substance in Psychology." *Bulletin, British Psychological Society* 34:265–270.

Lieberson, Jonathan. 1984. "Method Acting" [Review of W. G. Runciman, *A Treatise on Social Theory.* Vol. 1: *The Methodology of Social Theory.* Cambridge: Cambridge University Press, 1984]. *New York Review of Books* 31 (no. 17):45–50.

Lofland, John. 1971. *Analyzing Social Settings.* Belmont, Calif.: Wadsworth.

Lukács, Georg. 1971. *Writer & Critic.* New York: Grosset and Dunlap.

Luker, Kristin. 1975. *Taking Chances: Abortion and the Decision Not to Contracept.* Berkeley: University of California Press.

Maccoby, Eleanor E., and Nathan Maccoby. 1954. "The Interview: A Tool of Social Science." Chapter 12 in *Handbook of Social Psychology.* Vol. 1, *Theory and Method,* ed. Gardner Lindzey. Cambridge, Mass.: Addison-Wesley.

MacIntyre, Alasdair. 1981. *After Virtue.* Notre Dame, Ind.: University of Notre Dame Press.

Malcolm, Janet. 1983. "Six Roses ou Cirrhose?" [Review of Donald P. Spence, *Narrative Truth and Historical Truth: Meaning and Interpretation in Psychoanalysis.* New York: Norton, 1982]. *New Yorker,* January 24, pp. 96–105.

Mandler, Jean M. 1983. "What a Story Is." *Behavioral and Brain Sciences* 6:603–604.

———. 1984. *Stories, Scripts, and Scenes: Aspects of Schema Theory.* Hillsdale, N.J.: Lawrence Erlbaum Associates.

Mandler, Jean M., and Nancy S. Johnson. 1977. "Remembrance of Things Parsed: Story Structure and Recall." *Cognitive Psychology* 9:111–151.

———. 1980. "On Throwing Out the Baby with the Bathwater: A Reply to Black and Wilensky's Evaluation of Story Grammars." *Cognitive Science* 4:305–312.

McAdams, Don P. 1985. *Power, Intimacy, and the Life Story.* Homewood, Ill.: Dorsey Press.

Merton, Robert K., Marjorie Fiske, and Patricia L. Kendall. 1956. *The Focused Interview: A Manual of Problems and Procedures.* Glencoe, Ill.: Free Press.

Michaels, Sarah. 1981. " 'Sharing Time': Children's Narrative Styles and Differential Access to Literacy." *Language in Society* 10: 423–442.

———. 1983. "Influences on Children's Narratives." *Quarterly Newsletter of the Laboratory of Comparative Human Cognition* 5 (no. 2):30–34.

———. 1985. "Hearing the Connections in Children's Oral and Written Discourse." *Journal of Education* 167:36–56.

Michaels, Sarah, and Courtney B. Cazden. 1984. "Teacher-Child Collaboration as Oral Preparation for Literacy." In *Acquisition of Literacy: Ethnographic Perspectives,* ed. B. B. Schieffelin. Norwood, N.J.: Ablex.

Mies, Maria. 1983. "Towards a Methodology for Feminist Research." In *Theories of Women's Studies,* ed. Gloria Bowles and Renate D. Klein. London: Routledge & Kegan Paul.

Mishler, Anita L. 1978–80. "Cohort 1982." Unpublished study proposal, interviews, reports.

Mishler, Elliot G. 1975a. "Studies in Dialogue and Discourse: An Exponential Law of Successive Questioning." *Language in Society* 4:31–51.

———. 1975b. "Studies in Dialogue and Discourse: II. Types of Discourse Initiated and Sustained Through Questioning." *Journal of Psycholinguistic Research* 4:99–121.

———. 1978. "Studies in Dialogue and Discourse: III. Utterance Structure and Utterance Function in Interrogative Sequences." *Journal of Psycholinguistic Research* 7:279–305.

———. 1979. "Meaning in Context: Is There Any Other Kind?" *Harvard Educational Review* 49 (no. 1):1–19.

———. 1984. *The Discourse of Medicine: Dialectics of Medical Interviews.* Norwood, N.J.: Ablex.

———. 1986. "The Analysis of Interview Narratives." In *Narrative Psychology: The Storied Nature of Human Conduct,* ed. Theodore R. Sarbin. New York: Praeger.

Mishler, Elliot G., and Anita L. Mishler. 1976. "Marital Relationships at Midlife." Unpublished study proposal and interview schedule.

Molenaar, Nico J. 1982. "Response-effects of 'Formal' Characteristics of Questions." Chapter 3 in *Response Behavior in the Survey Interview,* ed. W. Dijkstra and J. van der Zouwen. New York: Academic Press.

Moss, Louis, and Harvey Goldstein, eds. 1979. *The Recall Method in Social Surveys.* Studies in Education 9. London: University of London Institute of Education.

Oakley, Ann. 1981. "Interviewing Women: A Contradiction in Terms." In *Doing Feminist Research.* ed. Helen Roberts. Boston: Routledge & Kegan Paul.

Ong, Walter J. 1982. "Oral Remembering and Narrative Structures." In *Analyzing Discourse: Text and Talk,* ed. Deborah Tannen. Washington, D.C.: Georgetown University Press.

Osherson, Samuel D. 1980. *Holding On or Letting Go.* New York: Free Press.

Paget, Marianne A. 1982. "Your Son Is Cured Now; You May Take Him Home." *Culture, Medicine and Psychiatry* 6:237–259.

———. 1983a. "Experience and Knowledge." *Human Studies.* 67–90.

———. 1983b. "On the Work of Talk: Studies in Misunderstandings." In *The Social Organization of Doctor-Patient Communication.* ed. Sue Fisher and Alexandra D. Todd. Washington, D.C.: Center for Applied Linguistics.

Peirce, Charles S. 1955. *Philosophical Writings of Peirce,* ed. Justus Buchler. New York: Harcourt, Brace.

Plummer, Ken. 1983. *Documents of Life: An Introduction to the Problems and Literature of a Humanistic Method.* Boston: George Allen & Unwin.

Polanyi, Livia. 1981. "What Stories Can Tell Us about Their Teller's World." *Poetics Today* 2:97–112.

―――. 1985. *Telling the American Story: A Structural and Cultural Analysis of Conversational Storytelling.* Norwood, N.J.: Ablex.

Presser, Stanley. 1983. "Review Essay: Survey Research Methodology versus Survey Research Practice." *Contemporary Sociology* 12: 636–639.

Propp, V. [1928] 1968. *Morphology of the Folktale,* 2nd ed. Austin: University of Texas Press.

Randall, Frederika. 1984. "Why Scholars Become Storytellers." *New York Times Book Review,* November 29, pp. 1, 31.

Rayfield, J. R. 1972. "What Is a Story?" *American Anthropologist* 74:1084–1106.

Ricoeur, Paul. 1981. *Hermeneutics and the Human Sciences.* Cambridge: Cambridge University Press.

Riesman, David, and Mark Benney. 1955. "The Sociology of the Interview." *Midwest Sociologist,* pp. 3–15.

―――. 1956. "Asking and Answering." *Journal of Business of the University of Chicago* 29:225–236.

Riessman, Catherine K. 1977. "Interviewer Effects in Psychiatric Epidemiology: A Study of Medical and Lay Interviewers and Their Impact on Reported Symptoms." Ph.D. diss, Columbia University, New York.

Robinson, W. P. 1972. *Language and Social Behavior.* Harmondsworth: Penguin Books.

Rosenwald, George C. 1985. "Hypocrisy, Self-Deception, and Perplexity: The Subject's Enhancement as Methodological Criterion." *Journal of Personality and Social Psychology* 49:682–703.

Rumelhart, David E. 1975. "Notes on a Schema for Stories." In *Representation and Understanding: Studies in Cognitive Science.* ed. Daniel G. Bobrow and Allan Collins. New York: Academic Press.

―――. 1977. "Understanding and Summarizing Brief Stories." In *Reading: Perception and Comprehension,* ed. David Leberge and S. Jay Samuels. Hillsdale, N.J.: Lawrence Erlbaum Associates.

―――. 1980. "On Evaluating Story Grammars." *Cognitive Science* 4:313–316.

Ryave, Alan L. 1978. "On the Achievement of a Series of Stories." Chapter 4 in *Studies in the Organization of Conversational Interaction,* ed. Jim Schenkein. New York: Academic Press.

Sacks, Harvey. 1972. "On the Analyzability of Stories by Children." Chapter 11 in *Directions in Sociolinguistics: The Ethnography of Com-*

munication. ed. John J. Gumperz and Dell Hymes. New York: Holt, Rinehart and Winston.

Sacks, Harvey. 1978. "Some Technical Considerations of a Dirty Joke." In *Studies in the Organization of Conversational Interaction,* ed. Jim Schenkein. New York: Academic Press.

Sacks, Harvey, Emmanuel A. Schegloff, and Gail Jefferson. 1974. "A Simplest Systematics for the Organization of Turn Taking for Conversation." *Language* 40:696–735.

Sarbin, Theodore R. 1983. "The Narrative as a Root Metaphor for Psychology." Paper presented to meetings of the American Psychological Association.

Sarbin, Theodore R. ed. 1986. *Narrative Psychology: The Storied Nature of Human Conduct.* New York: Praeger.

Schafer, Roy. 1980. "Narration in the Psychoanalytic Dialogue." *Critical Inquiry* 7:29–53.

———. 1983. *The Analytic Attitude.* New York: Basic Books.

Schegloff, Emmanuel A., and Harvey Sacks. 1973. "Opening Up Closings." *Semiotica* 8:289–327.

Scholes, Robert. 1980. "Afterthoughts on Narrative: Language, Narrative, and Anti-Narrative." *Critical Inquiry* 7:204–212.

Scholes, Robert, and Robert Kellogg. 1966. *The Nature of Narrative.* New York: Oxford University Press.

Schuman, Howard. 1982. "Artifacts Are in the Mind of the Beholder." *American Sociologist* 17:21–28.

Schuman, Howard, and Stanley Presser. 1981. *Questions and Answers in Attitude Surveys: Experiments on Question Form, Wording, and Content.* New York: Academic Press.

Scollon, Ron, and Suzanne B. K. Scollon. 1981. *Narrative, Literacy, and Face in Interethnic Communication.* Norwood, N.J.: Ablex.

Secord, Paul F., ed. 1982. *Explaining Human Behavior.* Beverly Hills, Calif.: Sage.

Smith, Barbara Herrnstein. 1980. "Narrative Versions, Narrative Theories." *Critical Inquiry* 7:212–236.

Smith, Dorothy E. 1983. "No One Commits Suicide: Textual Analysis of Ideological Practices." *Human Studies* 6:309–359.

Spence, Donald P. 1982. *Narrative Truth and Historical Truth: Meaning and Interpretation in Psychoanalysis.* New York: Norton.

Survey Research Center. 1976. *Interviewer's Manual,* rev. ed. Ann Arbor Institute for Social Research, University of Michigan.

Sutton-Smith, Brian. 1981. *The Folkstories of Children.* Philadelphia: University of Pennsylvania Press.

Sutton-Smith, Brian, Gilbert Botvin, and Daniel Mahony. 1976. "Developmental Structures in Fantasy Narratives." *Human Development* 19:1–13.

Tagg, Stephen K. 1985. "Life Story Interviews and Their Interpretation." In *The Research Interview: Uses and Approaches,* ed. Michael Brenner, Jennifer Brown, and David Canter. New York: Academic Press.

Tannen, Deborah, ed. 1982. *Analyzing Discourse: Text and Talk.* Georgetown University Roundtable on Languages and Linguistics, 1981. Washington, D.C.: Georgetown University Press.

Tedlock, Dennis. 1974. "Learning to Listen: Oral History as Poetry." In *Envelopes of Sound,* ed. Ronald J. Grele. Chicago: Precedent Publishing.

———. 1979. "The Analogical Tradition and the Emergence of a Dialogical Anthropology." *Journal of Anthropological Research* 35:387–400. Reprinted in Tedlock, 1983.

———. 1983. *The Spoken Word and the Work of Interpretation.* Philadelphia: University of Pennsylvania Press.

Thompson, Paul. 1978. *The Voice of the Past: Oral History.* Oxford: Oxford University Press.

———. 1981. "Life Histories and the Analysis of Social Change." In *Biography and Society: The Life History Approach in the Social Sciences,* ed. Daniel Bertaux. Beverly Hills, Calif.: Sage.

Trow, George W. S. 1981. *Within the Context of No Context.* Boston: Little, Brown.

Turner, Charles F. 1984. "Why Do Surveys Disagree? Some Preliminary Hypotheses and Some Disagreeable Examples." In *Surveying Subjective Phenomena,* vol. 2, ed. Charles F. Turner and Elizabeth Martin. New York: Russell Sage Foundation.

Turner, Charles F., and Elizabeth Martin, eds. 1984. *Surveying Subjective Phenomena,* 2 vols. New York: Russell Sage Foundation.

Turner, Victor. 1980. "Social Dramas and Stories about Them." *Critical Inquiry* 7:141–168.

Veroff, Joseph. 1983. "Contextual Determinants of Personality." *Personality and Social Psychology Bulletin* 9:331–343.

Veroff, Joseph, Elizabeth Douvan, and Richard A. Kulka. 1981. *The Inner American: A Self-Portrait from 1957 to 1976.* New York: Basic Books.

White, Hayden. 1973. *Metahistory: The Historical Imagination in Nineteenth-Century Europe.* Baltimore. Johns Hopkins University Press.

————. 1980. "The Value of Narrativity in the Representation of Reality." *Critical Inquiry* 7:5–27.

Wilensky, Robert. 1983. "Story Grammars versus Story Points [with commentaries]." *Behavioral and Brain Sciences* 6:579–623.

Willis, Paul E. 1977. *Learning to Labour.* Westmead, England: Saxon House.

Wolfson, Nessa. 1976. "Speech Events and Natural Speech: Some Implications for Sociolinguistic Methodology." *Languages in Society* 5: 189–209.

Yarrow, M. R., and C. Z. Waxler. 1979. "Observing Interaction: A Confrontation with Methodology." In *The Analysis of Social Interaction Methods, Issues and Illustrations,* ed. R. B. Cairns. Hillsdale, N.J.: Lawrence Erlbaum Associates.

Index